Advance Praise for Dancing in God's Earthquake

"The Jewish people's most revolutionary theologian is at it again, trying to waken us out of our moral slumber, before it is too late. The ancient prophet said: 'A lion roars? Who will not fear?' Waskow is our roaring lion." **—Rabbi Arthur Green, Rector of Rabbinical School at Hebrew College, author, *Judaism for the World***

"With this holy interbreathing, its 'Yyyyhhhwwwhhh,' its Breath of Life and Wind of change—you begin, we begin, to catch our own deepest breath. Whatever our religion or spirituality, we need Reb Waskow's teaching now more than ever. For this time of asphyxiations—social, racial, pandemic, and planetary, I cannot imagine a more important, more joyously activating and gorgeously readable, book." **—Catherine Keller, Drew University, author, *Political Theology of the Earth***

"Arthur Waskow is a true visionary. In *Dancing in God's Earthquake*, the metaphor of dancing is how he describes our relationship with change and with religious understanding. As we change, what we see in Torah and the Tanach changes. He imagines a new kind of society, far more cooperative with a respectful relationship with earth and all the other beings who inhabit it with us, always grounding his ideas in Judaism and in modern politics and evolving gender roles and identities." **—Marge Piercy**

"We tend to look at the earth as being solid, rock-like, and unchanging. But the truth of the matter is that there are times—like an earthquake—that what is under our feet shifts, moves, and glides. Those are times of tremendous opening, and possible destruction. Our own age feels like this. But Rabbi Waskow also holds out that rare, prophetic quality for us: Hope that the earthquake of our religious and spiritual traditions may also be an opening, a transformation, and a willingness to make of this whole world a new world. May it be so." **—Omid Safi, author, *Radical Love*; Director, Illuminated Tours**

"Like a true prophet, Rabbi Waskow looks with unapologetic eyes at both Scripture and this historical moment, weaving them into a spiral of meaning that informs each with depth and inspired imagination. He encourages us to engage our world fully and authentically, inviting us to grow up as a species and take our place within the wisdom of Creation. *Dancing in God's Earthquake* teaches us the dance of Breathing with all beings to the rhythm of a changing, exciting, and beautiful world." **—Anne Symens-Bucher, Co-founder, Canticle Farm, Oakland, CA**

"Rabbi Arthur Waskow unapologetically thinks and acts outside of the box of conventional wisdom, fueled by his unwavering commitment to love and compassion affirmed by blood, sweat, and tears. He is a righteous renegade in a world steeped in corruption, demanding change." **—Imam Al-Hajj Talib 'Abdur-Rashid, author, *Social Justice Writings of an American Muslim of African Descent***

"For decades, Arthur Waskow has tapped the creative imagination of the human community to challenge systems of domination and injustice. *Dancing in God's Earthquake* continues that challenge, setting the stage for a radical and hopeful theological journey that may well pull us all into the dance!" **—Marie Dennis, Senior Advisor and Former Co-President, Pax Christi International**

"Reb Arthur Waskow is a prophet among us. He channels both the wisdom and the outrage of ancient voices in a modern call to action. People of all faiths, and people of no faiths will all be called to this sacred dance. **—Rabbi Jonah Pesner, director, Religious Action Center of Reform Judaism**

DANCING IN GOD'S EARTHQUAKE

The Coming Transformation of Religion

Rabbi Arthur Ocean Waskow

Founded in 1970, Orbis Books endeavors to publish works that enlighten the mind, nourish the spirit, and challenge the conscience. The publishing arm of the Maryknoll Fathers and Brothers, Orbis seeks to explore the global dimensions of the Christian faith and mission, to invite dialogue with diverse cultures and religious traditions, and to serve the cause of reconciliation and peace. The books published reflect the views of their authors and do not represent the official position of the Maryknoll Society. To learn more about Maryknoll and Orbis Books, please visit our website at http://www.maryknollsociety.org.

Published by Orbis Books, Box 302, Maryknoll, NY 10545-0302.

Manufactured in the United States of America.

Library of Congress Cataloging-in-Publication Data

Names: Waskow, Arthur Ocean, 1933– author.
Title: Dancing in God's earthquake : the coming transformation of religion / Rabbi Arthur Ocean Waskow.
Description: Maryknoll, NY : Orbis Books, 2020.
Identifiers: LCCN 2020009354 (print) | LCCN 2020009355 (ebook) | ISBN 9781626984004 (trade paperback) | ISBN 9781608338641 (ebook)
Subjects: LCSH: Religion—History—21st century. | Spirituality—History—21st century. | Religions—History—21st century.
Classification: LCC BL98 .W375 2020 (print) | LCC BL98 (ebook) | DDC 200.9/05—dc23
LC record available at https://lccn.loc.gov/2020009354
LC ebook record available at https://lccn.loc.gov/2020009355

A Blessing

Before we begin learning with each other how to reinterpret and apply ancient wisdom to our own lives, we are taught to say a blessing. The blessing reminds us that study and thought are not ends in themselves; they are intended to guide us toward action to make a world wiser.

Long ago a group of rabbis hid in an attic from the Roman Empire's army—for Rome had decreed death for either study of Torah or acts of Torah. They debated amongst themselves: "Should we rather risk our lives for study or for action?"

The great Rabbi Akiba ended the debate: "Which is greater, study or action? Study if it leads to action!" And the sages agreed.

So here is the blessing, slightly transmuted and translated to lift up the wisdom of our own time:

> Blessed are You, Interbreathing Spirit of all life, for You breathe life into us, You breathe into us the awareness that our breath is stirred by Yours, You breathe into us the impulse to shape our breath into words, and You breathe into us the desire to shape our words so

> that they aim toward wisdom, stirring us to deeds that
> make sacred loving connection with all life.

At the end of this book, this guide to dancing in God's earthquake, there will be a companion blessing to complete our sacred conversation and to begin the dance.

For my beloved comrade

In teaching and learning,

In writing and speaking,

In politics and play,

In living and loving;

Who also in her own lives was and is

Both self-transforming and transforming of the world.

Rabbi Phyllis Ocean Berman

When Godwrestlers went free

from the Tight and Narrow Place,

The sea looked and fled;

Rivers flowed backward.

Mountains danced like rams,

the hills like lambs.

What, O Sea, does make you flee?

O Rivers, why reverse your flow?

O Mountains, that you dance like rams?

O Hills, like lambs?

Quake, O Earth!

Before the Holy Presence

Who transforms Jacob into Yisrael—

"Heel-Grabber" into "Godwrestler"—

The rock into a pool of water,

Flint into wellspring.

—Psalm 114

Contents

A Note to the Reader

Coronavirus: The Eleventh Plague

On November 13, 2019, I emailed the text of *Dancing in God's Earthquake* to Robert Ellsberg, the publisher of Orbis Books. On December 4, I heard back: "Short answer: *I love your book*."

In late December 2019, the first reports began to reach the outside world of a troublesome new virus striking people in Wuhan, China.

I note this sequence of events to explain why the word "coronavirus" is not mentioned in this book. And yet throughout the text, this "earthquake" among all the earthquakes in our lives—the life of all Humanity—is ever-present, even if invisible and inaudible. The ancient rabbis taught that Torah was written not in black ink on white parchment but in black fire on white fire—and we must read the fiery "blank" white spaces by interpretation of the whole intent. This prefatory note is a tiny, inky wakening of the in-between white spaces of this book. I invite you to read not only this but whatever sparks of meaning rise for you from all the other white spaces that await you.

In the ancient biblical tradition, there comes a story of a profound earthquake in the life of *Am Yisrael*—the people that chose to name itself the Godwrestlers. That is the story of the Exodus from slavery in the country that in Hebrew is named *Mitzrayyim,* "Tight Narrow Place" (in English "Egypt"). The Exodus moves into a freely wandering, struggling, learning, growing journey in a Wilderness, seeking to become a loving and beloved community.

The Exodus is empowered by a series of Ten Plagues. In many understandings, they were brought on by a God Who is a sort of Super-Pharaoh in the sky, proving he is even more powerful and more cruel than the Pharaoh on the Egyptian throne, who claims to be a god. Pharaoh enslaves Israelites; God kills Egyptians.

This understanding that the Exodus is a contest between a king and a Super-King is underlined by the false biblical translation of *YHWH* as "LORD." (The rabbinic tradition substituted "*Adonai*/Lord" for "YHWH" but the Hebrew Bible does not.) It is more likely that *YHWH* with no vowels is simply a breath—Yyyyyhhhhhwwwwwhhhh: the Breath of life, sometimes the Wind of change, sometimes the Hurricane of destruction.

This *Ruach* (Hebrew for "breath, wind, spirit") is what intertwines all life. We know now this is literally, physically, scientifically true: the Oxygen-CO2 interbreathing between animals and vegetation keeps all life alive. So *YHWH* is the bearer of consequence, not punishment or rewards. Try reading the whole Plague narrative substituting "Interbreath of life" instead of "LORD." For me and others who have tried this, it changes the whole story.

From this vantage point, the story describes the concentrated power and the arrogance, cruelty, and stubbornness of a Pharaoh whose subjugation of human beings soon became subjugation of Earth. Undrinkable water. Impossibly intrusive frogs (according to ancient rabbinic midrash, even inside human bodies). Boils. Mad cow disease. Hordes of locusts, swallowing up all food crops. Unprecedented hailstorms, flashes of fire kindling and burning trees in orchards and in forests. Darkness so thick that human beings became invisible to each other. And more—ultimately, the death of first-borns in every Egyptian family.

Though the ancient plagues were the horrifying results of Pharaoh's cruelty, they became the instruments of liberation.

How could both truths be true? The Exodus story splits the targets of the plagues. For Egyptians, they were utterly destructive. For Israelites, who according to the story were physically and ecologically separated in their own region of Goshen, they were liberating. Whether the separation was factually accurate or a part of a larger parable, it was a way of celebrating the emergence of a new kind of community. That community was committed to a new birth of freedom. Yet it was open, as the story of Pharaoh's daughter tells us, to "renegade refugees" even from the palace of privilege and power.

We, living in the midst of the Coronavirus Plague and the varied plagues of global scorching, do not have the luxury of regional separation. Our own "Goshen" is retreat into our own homes, scattered everywhere. Our own new plagues imposed by modern pharaohs are again horrifying and might-be liberating: Undrinkable water. Intrusive "forever plastics," even inside human bodies. Droughts. Famines. Floods. Fires. Human beings becoming unable to see each other through the darkness of fear. Ultimately, the dangerously impending death of the next generation of the human species—our own first- and second- and tenth-borns.

Our new plagues *might* be sounding the death-knell of an old world order of Domination and Hierarchy. Or they might, by making uprising for freedom so difficult to do in public and by destroying jobs and workplaces, reinforce the power of our pharaohs until all of us are conscripted into the chariot army that drowns in the Sea of misery, despair, and death.

Which future is our future depends on us. Can we suffer from the plagues and yet—and therefore!—act on them as birth-cries of a new worldview of ecological interwovenness: seeing our communities of life as conscious interconnected ecosystems of biology, culture, and society—rooted in love and flowering in life-affirming justice?

As I write, in early April 2020, on the verge of the Passover that tells the story of ten Plagues of liberation, we are suffering from the Eleventh Plague, the new coronavirus. It is not the only plague that is afflicting all Humanity—and some of the others are afflicting not only Humankind but a million other species as well as the air and oceans of all Earth.

Today political "leaders" in a number of different nations are so addicted to their own power and glory, so much like the ancient pharaoh, that at first they treated medical warnings about the new coronavirus as "hoaxes." They imposed hush and hesitation when they should have been calling, loud and urgent, for vigorous healing action.

Months-long official lies and pretense have already sentenced many Chinese, Italians, Iranians, and Americans to death by virus. Decades-long lies and refusals to respond to climate warnings have already sent thousands of people to their deaths by heatstroke in Europe; droughts in Syria and Central America; fires in Australia and California; and floods in Central Africa and Puerto Rico, New Orleans and New York.

The delays in facing the virus gave it a head start in America. That head start led to swift viral spread, and as contagion grew and deaths multiplied, then to stringent prohibitions against physical presence at work or in community.

At just the precisely right and utterly uncanny moment, the Jewish calendar of Torah readings addressed how to deal with individuals or whole communities that could not be fully and physically present in the broader sacred community because they had been in contact with a human death. The Torah taught an intricate ritual of the "red heifer" to release them into rejoining the broader community.

In that passage (Numbers 19) the ritual of reconnection began with the burning of a red heifer—its red skin, red blood, and red flesh all visible—in a red fire made still more red by casting into it a scarlet dye. The Hebrew word for "red" in this passage is "*adumah*." It echoes the words *adamah* for earth and *adam* for human earthling. Both words also have "red" at their roots. When human beings die (from earth we came, to earth we return), *Adam* melts back into the *adamah*: death is an uncanny redness. To touch this death or to touch someone who has touched this death plunges us into this uncanny red amalgam. It takes a deep plunge into a similar but different redness, a fiery redness, to begin releasing us to life again.

And the plunge is not just verbal, a deadly serious pun. The Bible says this spectacle of redness was done "for the eyes of the priests." Perhaps this hinted at the truth that if we stare into a red intensity and then blink, our closed eyes see a flash of green—the color of life growing. If we gaze into Death unflinching and only then transform the sight by blinking, our eyes will show us Life.

The ashes of the burnt red heifer were mixed into water; the living humans who had touched this death needed to plunge into this water on the third and seventh days afterward. Then they could reenter communal sacred space.

That passage came up for reading in mid-March 2020, just as "isolation" from communal gatherings was becoming the law of the land. On that Shabbat I led a Torah-study group that I have led for years, only this time at a distance, through Zoom. I found myself thinking that Zoom—followed by repeated hand-washings—was our "red heifer," allowing us to reenter loving and prayerful community, even when physically we can't, overwhelmed as we are by our own contact with death.

When we do return to physical connection with our communities, God forbid that we simply rejoice in the passing of this crisis. And God forbid that we learn nothing, turning our eyes, our ears, our hearts, and our heads away.

During the struggle to end the Vietnam War, Howard Zinn told me that for most of our lives, we walk in the dark. The jagged edges of our society may stab and bloody us, but we cannot see them. The war then became, and this moment now has become, a lightning-flash to light up our reality and its failings. Let us emblazon onto our brains what we saw in that moment, so that we can act to heal ourselves, not fall back into a fake nostalgia.

What we can learn from the coronavirus crisis:

- We really are one planet. Even prohibitions on "foreign" travel have mostly been too late to prevent transnational contagion. This is true even when human travel is the carrier. Can we translate that knowledge to even stronger cases, like the unity of our dangerously and recklessly overheated atmosphere and oceans affecting the whole planet?
- Governments, businesses, and families *can* move swiftly for profound change when sufficiently motivated. Many of them at first respond antidemocratically, with silence and lies. They may take serious action only when public outcry cannot be silenced and their own power becomes precarious.
- We *can* respond to the climate crisis, as we did to the coronavirus crisis, most effectively by engaging more people in active political struggle. For examples: More effort to fill our activism itself with love, celebration, and community. More engagement by religious communities, especially each year as we approach Passover and Holy Week. New forms of interconnection, like solar co-ops and change-insistent groups that celebrate

together (online and in person). Increasing our direct challenge to governments that they will lose power if they don't respond to the climate plagues as vigorously as they have to the coronavirus plague.

- Protection for the most vulnerable has become a political issue but not yet a political given. (How do the homeless "self-isolate" without homes? How do hourly paid workers choose to stay home and keep themselves and others safe and healthy, if they have no paid sick leave and no health insurance? How do children whose only daily bread is a school lunch eat when schools are closed? How do asylum-seekers stay healthy when they are packed into filthy detention centers or forced into jammed vehicles and sent back to tent cities? And prisoners and guards in way-overcrowded prisons?)
- Perhaps the most obvious lesson of all: We must have universal health care. There are many different ways to get there, as many different countries have found. Get there we must.
- We must make sure that special government and other aid goes also to those displaced and disemployed people who are worst affected by the coronavirus crisis and by the corporate Carbon poisoning of air and water, and most hurt by sudden great shifts in the economy.
- While "social distancing" must go on long enough to make sure that the process of contagion has been halted, we must, as soon as possible, make sure that we do not make social distance or some other cramping of our lives into a habit. The isolation of our bodies from each other is dangerous to our souls and to the soul of democracy. The open society has to take place in open workplaces, open homes of prayer and Spirit, open visits to open government offices, open vigils and protest rallies, open hugs and handshakes.

- Long before a crisis, a long-view imagination and approach to planning are necessary. Starving an agency so that it can barely meet immediate needs—as much of our public health system was starved—leaves it helpless to address an unplanned, unexpected emergency.
- When deep change does happen, along with death and danger it may swiftly bring forth its own unexpected rewards. The sky above Wuhan, dirty and smoggy for decades, has become blue again during the Great Pause. The waters of Venice, long impenetrably muddy, have become once again transparent during the Great Pause. Though the first motive for the Pause was fear, many people are reporting that the social responses are filled with love and a desire to strengthen community even as social distancing strains it. Having once again tasted these joyful values, we can try to bring them to our tables beyond the crisis.

By the time this book is in your hands, you will know how many of us have so far learned these lessons. Writing in March 2020, I can't know now. But I know this much: we can make this Great Pause a restful, just, and joyful Shabbat—even perhaps several sabbatical months.

And somewhere, sometime, as with the weekly and the seventh-year Shabbat, we must take up the joy and justice-seeking of honorable work for good lives and livelihoods, in physical communities of work as well as celebration. We must integrate into the fullness of our ongoing lives what we have learned from this moment.

What did we learn? That all Earth and all Humanity are intertwined, a Grand Ecosystem connected by the Breath of Life and tinged with Divinity—and that efforts by any part to subjugate the rest will destroy us all.

An Overture to the Dance

We are all living through a world earthquake. Not only hills and mountains, rivers and oceans are dancing in the earthquake, as Psalm 114 foresaw. Every human community is quaking. Every aspect of our lives is shaking under foot and in our bellies—political, sexual, familial, intellectual, medical, military, economic, ecological. And some of us are trying to learn how to dance.

I know from earthquakes. I lived through the earthquake of the murder of Dr. Martin Luther King, and I learned to dance into a new me, even while—especially while—the "dance floor" itself was dancing in the earthquake of 1968.

I have learned that when I weave a deep conversation where our words can aim toward wisdom, the way to begin is to look inward, beyond even the wisest of texts, and only then to dance and wrestle with the texts.

So I invite you, Reader, to begin this book by looking inward—right here, right now. What aspect of the "worldquake" have you faced—in your family and friends, your body, your sexuality, your faith, your livelihood, your experience of violence, of calm? How did you feel—literally feel, in your bones and in your belly? In your breath? Let yourself feel that way again, for just a minute.

* * *

Come back to Now, to your conversation with me. It is words we will share—words that long before they were printed on paper or electrons were Breath, shaped by our lips and tongue as we spoke them with each other. I invite you to pause to feel how your breath comes to you from trees and grasses, how it moves through you and then moves out to trees and grasses. This interbreathing, multiplied many trillion times, keeps all life on Earth, in Earth, alive.

We pause to thank that Breath: You/We/I breathe into us our consciousness of you, our consciousness that we are part of You, that you breathe into us the impulse to shape Your breath into words and the desire to shape our words so that they aim toward wisdom.

What arose for me in recalling my own Earthquake?

My own life was transformed by the week between the murder of Dr. Martin Luther King and the first night of Passover in 1968. The violent victory of racism over the most effective and beloved nonviolent leader in American history was followed by uprisings in Black communities across the country. They were followed by repressive police responses and even military occupations of some cities—including Washington DC, the capital of the United States, where I lived.

One week after Dr. King was murdered, the coming of Passover brought me "awoke." The moment of "awokening" came when I walked home to prepare for my family's Passover Seder, retelling the story of the liberation of the ancient Israelites from slavery under Pharaoh. As I approached my home, I saw a Jeep with a machine gun pointed at the block I lived on.

From deep in my gut arose the words "This is Pharaoh's Army, and I am going home to do the Seder. This is Pharaoh's Army."

That moment was the turning of my life.

To what did I awake? To an earthquake inside me and an earthquake all around me. Within me, the earthquake shook me first into transforming my understanding of Passover. From a pleasant memorial in words and foods and melodies of an ancient Jewish freedom struggle, it became a beckoning, an incitement, to all peoples now to win their freedom from all Pharaohs; and I found myself writing a new version of the ancient Telling—a Freedom *Seder*, we called it.

Soon the earthquake shook me into transforming my whole life, from a barely casual relationship with being Jewish to a passionate encounter with Jewish thought and practice. I found myself, beyond my will, reframing my life around Jewish teachings, symbols, festivals, and practices—ultimately, to becoming a rabbi.

Around me, the earthquake of 1968 exploded the Democratic National Convention in Chicago—where I was a delegate —into a fiasco. Its failure showed that American democracy was incapable of ending the racism that murdered Dr. King and tore our cities apart. And incapable of ending the war that was tearing our country apart.

And even before Dr. King's death, the first tremors of earthquake had begun to shake the ultimate institutions of solidity and calm—the churches and synagogues whose very purpose had been to assure everyone that the world was well put together.

So my own inner earthquake did not send me into joining the Judaism of my childhood, the Judaism of the last two thousand years, or the Judaism I could see all around me. My earthquake did not drive me into hanging on to some immovable past. Instead, I began to connect to the broken fragments of the old Tablets of Certainty as the fragments began to glow and glimmer new thoughts, new patterns.

I began dancing my way into a new version of Judaism. And I learned how to do that and in the same breath, the same dance, to swoop and turn with other traditions, other symbols, other festivals.

Along the way, the continuing shaking of America and of the world, even the biological Earth, also brought me dancing to a new way of understanding God. Not "Lord," "King," up there lording it over us poor *shleppers* here beneath. Rather, the Interbreathing Spirit of all life. The Great Name in which is woven all the names of all the beings in the universe.

"What is the world?" asked the Rebbe of Chernobyl, one of the great Hassidic teachers. "The world is God, wrapped in robes of God so as to appear to be material. And who are we? We are God, wrapped in robes of God, and our task is to unwrap the robes, discover—uncover—that we and all the world are God."

It is in that sense that I see our earthquake as God's earthquake. The Breathing Spirit of all life has become not just a Breath, not only the Wind of Change, but the Hurricane of Transformation. The Transformation, the Earthquake, is what we make, what we live, what we are.

In 1968 I was not alone. Indeed, the year 1968 in America and France and Czechoslovakia became a moment when shock after shock became an earthquake. And half a century later, the world is still shaking in every dimension of our being. What do we do when the earth keeps quaking, when we begin to realize it is not a momentary lapse?

Some of us stagger along, helpless, falling, being clobbered, even dying as the planet trembles. We try to carry on business—"busyness"—as usual. Our keeping busy in our accustomed patterns distracts us from the vast changes going on around us. Anyway, we don't know what else to do. If the world is toppling, we can still keep doing what we already know how to do.

Some of us look desperately for something immovable that we might be able to hang onto while the world shakes. We may look to a photograph we carry in our heads from the "orderly" past. (The photo may in fact be fuzzy and untruthful, but better this past "certainty" than so much disorder in the present.) That immovable past has in it power structures of the soul, the psyche, and society: The patriarchal family. Contempt for queers. America's "manifest destiny" to control the world. The subordination of women. Acceptance of a world in which the wealthy have the strongest voice and tell us all how to behave. Acceptance of a norm in which some cultures, some religions, some communities, some races, are in charge and some obey.

And, of course, we celebrate religions as they were handed down to us, frozen into patterns that emerged when the last great earthquake calmed down. We may retell the stories of those earthquakes. We may retell the stories of how a Pharaoh or a Caesar fell from power in that earthquake. But most of those who teach us those stories insist that those tumultuous times are over. Our religious lives, they insist, must not be contaminated by a search for modern Pharaohs or Caesars, or by listening seriously to other religious traditions—let alone to the always unfolding Voice of God.

And then there is the third way of responding to the "worldquake" we are living through: learning to dance in the earthquake. It is hard to dance when the dance floor itself is dancing, shaking, whirling, changing shape. How can we bring grace, music, joy into that dancing? Hard—but that, it seems to me, is the most life-giving response to the world we live in.

For me, the writing and rewriting of this book, the living and reliving of an activist politics rooted in the Bible and the Spirit, have brought me to clarifying a new theology as well as a new politics. The new theology is ecological rather than hierarchical. I do not mean only a theology far more infused with Earth, but one that sees all life—the interweaving of organs to make a whole body–mind, the interweaving of cultures to make a whole Humanity—as deeply different from the model of the Great Chain of Being that saw rocks at the bottom of a chain of rising consciousness; vegetation one step up; various levels of animal life still higher; almost at the top, the human race; and just above, the Royal God, ruler of them all, Lord and King.

Instead, we are moving toward a vision of Reality and God that sees the species, the organs, the cultures intertwined, and *YHWH* as the Breath of Life that interbreathes us all. *YHWH* pronounced not as Yahweh or Jehovah or Adonai or Lord but as itself—*YyyyHhhhWwwwHhhh*, a Breathing that is experienced as one of the wisest organic metaphors for the Holy One.

And this shift accords with my own life-growth into hearing the Hebrew Bible as not only an anthology of diverse tales and sources but as itself a subtle Unity—a beckoning to the human race to grow up. From birth and infancy and childhood, from adolescence to an adulthood drenched in drudgery and domination, and beyond, toward a maturity of peaceful sharing of abundance.

This way of understanding the Bible's understanding of reality is quite different from the model that now dominates the work of "leftish" theologians. That model is one rooted in *tikkun*—the healing of a broken world. In that model, the world we all inherit is shattered. It is up to us to invent the tools we need to struggle to repair the broken vessel.

Seeing Humanity and all of life in a process of maturing does not endorse every choice we make as we grow. We make mistakes. From bad results and sour experience we learn to make wiser choices. The whole process can feel more joyful if that is what we understand we're doing, more joyful than if in anger we curse or knuckle under to "the Lord" who has handed us the down and dirty task of repairing "His" broken, misbegotten world.

Sometimes in our growing we make a giant choice so big and complicated that it is hard to disentangle success from bad mistake. That is when we find ourselves in an earthquake. God's Earthquake. And if we can keep in mind that the Earthquake comes because we have grown a few giant steps forward toward grown-upness, and simply need to pause, to catch our breath, and then to take another step—if we can keep that in mind, we can dance the next few steps instead of trudging them.

Some of us have had the individual experience of learning to dance to a new tune because an earthquake in our personal lives has erased the old melodies. Some of us have had our lives transformed by the earthquake in the whole social system we are part of.

This is not the first time whole societies have had to learn to dance in an earthquake.

About three thousand years ago, the pressure of two empires—Egyptian and Babylonian—imposed an earthquake on a loose network of Western Semitic communities. Out of the earthquake emerged a new kind of community, what we know as the biblical people of Israel—Torah, Shabbat, the Sabbatical Year, challenges to the existing rules of serfdom and enslavement and the subjugation of foreigners, provisions for rhythmic renewal of the earthy land itself, prophetic visions of universal peace despite a present in the midst of constant war.

About two thousand years ago, the suzerainty of Rome imposed an earthquake on the cultures of the Mediterranean basin. Out of the earthquake emerged two new kinds of communities—Rabbinic Judaism and Christianity.

Today, we live in an earthquake that is shaking all the previous cultures of the globe. Some of the changes seem to work for human advancement; others damage human beings and many other species. They began with the Industrial Revolution built on burning fossil fuels. From this came easily available newspapers and worldwide computer conversations; worldwide kidnapping of human beings into slavery and the subjugation of whole continents into colonies; newly successful medicines and effective birth control; far more food and many more human beings; mass democracies and efforts to guarantee human rights; the emancipation of slaves and colonies; academies of verifiable science, first in a reductionist take-it-apart mode and then taking seriously the interconnection of life-forms in an ecological worldview that spread beyond biology to cultures. And alongside these sweet-and-sour fruits there came some that were baleful, poisonous to all of Humankind: industrialized genocide, H-Bombs, and global scorching.

Some of these uncertain shuffling steps lifted our knowledge, our compassion; some multiplied cruelty. All of them together shook us into a worldwide earthquake. And perhaps into the slow emergence of new kinds of community: Renewing, transforming Judaism, Christianity, Islam, secularism, science, Hinduism, Buddhism. Making "interfaith" and "multireligious" connections and learnings that a century ago would have been labeled heresy. Renewing, transforming, what it means to be an American, a French (wo)man, an Israeli, a Palestinian, Indigenous. What it means to be a tree, a frog, a symbiotic biome in some human's belly. Not only transforming each community for the sake of its own future, but reshaping each so that all can connect with each other.

Out of suffering Pharaoh—Moses, Aaron, Miriam, Sinai.

Out of suffering Nebuchadnezzar—Isaiah, Jeremiah, Zechariah.

Out of suffering Rome—Akiba, Jesus, Mary, "The Thunder —Perfect Mind."

Out of suffering tyrannized Mecca—Mohammed.

Out of suffering the Holocaust, the H-Bomb, Trump, and

global scorching—Carson, MLK, Heschel, SNCC, Barber, the Dreamers, McKibben, Sarsour, Ocasio-Cortez.

And more? And more!

When I–It becomes unbearable, I–Thou flowers.

But never going back to an old form. Always drawing nourishment from the older wisdom, always learning something new from the noxious overlord, moving forward in a spiral.

Connecting with each other in this way is the social and political equivalent of an ecosystem, in which all our cultures interbreathe in joyful diversity in order to transform the world into a joyful home for human beings and all other life-forms.

In that respectful listening to and learning from all our cultures, I discovered—uncovered!—the unexpected truth that I owe a great deal to the culture of ancient Earth-oriented Judaism—the Hebrew Scriptures. They were the spiritual expression of what we would now call an indigenous people—shepherds and farmers in close touch with Earth.

Indeed, it seemed a historical near-miracle that this spiritual journal of an indigenous people survived as a treasure available to many peoples that were not at all "indigenous." In this crisis of the great Earthquake, we begin to realize that we have all become, as it were, "indigenous" peoples threatened by great empires of power, wealth, and technology. Suddenly events like the gathering of Native Nations at Standing Rock in the Dakotas to resist the destruction of their sacred waters and their sacred graves spoke to a public that for centuries had treated such cultures with contempt and subjugation. Could a worldwide people long riven from its land learn from that ancient wisdom a new approach to loving every land?

The "dancing" response to our earthquake is not the only one. If the world keeps shaking, even while we hang on to what we think that we remember, some of us may decide that the best we can do is try to make everyone else hang on to that fabled past as well. That may require some coercion, but orderly domination may seem better than sheer chaos.

Indeed, the more that some of us dance our way into new blessings that contravene old wisdom, the more others of us see our new dance as filled with deadly sins and put their strongest energy into preventing or punishing these sins defined of old.

There is no question that our traditions did define some acts as sinful. And so we may today. But which actions? And what are the criteria that underlie our decisions? For instance, the Bible commands us to "Be fruitful, multiply, fill up the Earth, and subdue it." Now that we are approaching eight billion humans on the planet, possessing nuclear weapons that could stop all photosynthesis and end all life, and using our sheer numbers and our CO_2 emissions to create the Sixth Great Extinction, have "Fill up the Earth" and "Subdue it" become a dangerous sin?

A precedent! The Talmud forbade raising sheep and goats in the Land of Israel. What chutzpah! How could the rabbis do this, seeing that herding was exactly the life practice of Abraham and Sarah, Isaac and Rebekah, and others of our sacred forebears? The rabbis realized that so many goats and sheep were munching on the grass that it would soon be denuded, bringing ruin on the Land and on the people. A blessing had become a sin.

The question is what defined those actions as sinful or blessing? If "sin" is what hurts people, forbidding it seems fair enough. So if ancient teaching says it is a sin to fail to pay our workers before the sun sets on the work they have been doing, that seems fair enough. (And millions of us responded that way when a partial shutdown of the US government in 2018 left hundreds of thousands of workers trapped without being paid for weeks.)

But is it possible for the great earthquake to shake our social and personal geography enough that some sinful acts that damaged people now actually meet their deepest needs? Become joyful blessings rather than sins?

For example, the Bible clearly thought it was a sin for two men to have sex. That may have had to do with wanting to "be fruitful, multiply and fill up the Earth" with children. It may have had to do with not wanting one man to subjugate another man "as with a woman," since it was considered normal, even desirable—certainly not a sin!—to subjugate women. Whatever the reason, we are living through an earthquake in which many of us have learned that sexuality has more joyful blessings than we realized: that two men, or two women, can create a joyful and sacred relationship. Now that our eyes have been shaken wider open by the earthquake, many of us can see love around us where before we could see only sin.

Indeed, many of the ancient sins that are invoked by those today who oppose new dances in the earthquake have to do with sexuality. The ancient definitions of those sins, especially in early Christianity, leaned heavily on fearing sex, subordinating women in part because they roused such intense anarchic feelings in the men who controlled the ancient narrative and wanted to control their own lives, not leave them subject to anarchic flashes. Even the metaphor of "dancing" might evoke such dangers.

Efforts toward equality of women and men in religious life and in society as a whole have undercut this focus on sexual sin, and have redefined what sin in our sexual lives may be: the abuse of power through rape and harassment, for example, have in some communities become seen as far more sinful than consensual sex out of wedlock. Even in religious communities that define most forms of birth control as sinful, 98 percent of the women in those communities do use those methods of birth control.

Since one response that many people have to our world earthquake is to hold fast the "immovable" communal patterns of the past, their impulse is to treat as sins any deviation from those patterns, even if the deviation is nurturing to many human beings. This dynamic sets up a difficult relationship between those who wish to "dance" new patterns when the landscape, the dance floor, itself is dancing, and those who think that safety lies in restoring the past.

Often the tension between restoration and transformation leads to forbidding a specific sin, invoking coercion to prevent or punish it if it seems to weaken a traditional community, even if it does not harm specific individuals. Then it becomes hard to reexamine what sin is, what sins are. Religions themselves may experience earthquakes, and the survival technique of holding fast to the past is especially strong when it comes to sin and coercion.

Perhaps the most obvious example of both resistance to change and wholesale adoption of change in the midst of earthquake is what happened to Judaism when it was shaken by Rome. In a few cases, some Jews faced the destruction of the Holy Temple in Jerusalem and being severed from the earthy land in which offerings of food had been the central way of approaching God by building sacrificial temples far away (Elephantine in Upper Egypt, for example). A much larger number of Jews responded by turning to words of prayer and words of Torah study as the heart of Jewish religious life.

My bias in this book is toward learning from the past but not restoring it. For this reason, I lean toward

- treating some actions that our ancient wisdom said were sins as, in our new world, bountiful blessings;
- treating some actions that were anciently described as blessings as having become sins under the new conditions that we live in; and
- realizing that some blessings that the Bible could only wistfully envision are now almost within our grasp—

achievable if we put our will and energy toward making them happen

One word about this third category: When Isaiah spoke eloquently of a world where nations will learn war no more, where all the swords will be beaten into plowshares, where the lion and the lamb will lie down peacefully together, he knew there was no way of actually achieving this in his lifetime. He was convinced it was important to set forth this unachievable vision, and we continue to honor his attempt.

In many of the chapters of this book, I will sketch projects that may at first seem beyond our reach. Some of them may be, but I hope they will set our visions in a life-giving direction. Others I believe can be accomplished if we will them.

Beginning after the joy of the Freedom Seder in 1969, once I grew beyond the shock of feeling myself drawn into not repeating but remaking a Judaism that I had previously ignored, I found myself learning from other cultures and traditions as well.

Almost fifty years ago, I heard Rabbi Zalman Schachter-Shalomi say that Rabbinic Judaism was finished, shattered by Modernity the way Biblical Judaism had been shattered by Rome. We were already beginning, he said, to shape a whole new paradigm of Judaism. And in June 2018, at a meeting of the Philadelphia Board of Rabbis, I heard Rabbi Steven Wernick, executive of the United Synagogue of Conservative Judaism, say exactly the same words. No one stood up to scream or wail.

In half a century, this assessment moved from the fringes of the fringes of the community, from a rabbi searching toward the unimaginable—a feminist neo-Hassidic Sinai—to the epicenter of American Jewish religious life. In half a century!

Let me be clear about why I feel drawn to write this book, to dance in the music of Torah rather than shrug it away.

First: After living through the murder of Dr. King and Passover, then the murder of Bobby Kennedy, and the disastrous "unfreedom" of being a delegate to the infamous Chicago Convention of the Democratic Party—a kind of devil's inversion of Passover—I could do no other. Passover and its inversion freed me into a new me by gripping me inexorably. "Inexorable" is, literally, what you cannot pray yourself out of. As I found myself drawn deeper and deeper into a Judaism that did not exist and cried out to be created, I felt the same inexorable gravitational pull.

Second, I began to experience deep wisdom in the biblical tradition: wisdom that had inspired hundreds of generations of people who had rewritten it, reinterpreted it, reenacted it. Something in its ability to dance bespoke a sacred music. Precisely because it did not fit inside the generations I was living through, I came to respect its importance to the generations I was living through—still *am* living through.

And I also found the listening went more ways than one. The more fully I learned the Jewish practice of *midrash*—twirling the ancient text to let it speak new wisdom—the more I found Christians, Muslims, and secularists opening their ears. What Christians often call the Old Testament is sacred to them, too. It also holds a special place in the Islamic worldview. And the Hebrew Scriptures—the story of Pharaoh and the Exodus, for example—have even had a strong impact on modern secularism. So I expect that my drawing on its stories will speak beyond the Jewish community.

In me and in us all, the alternatives of hold tight the past or dance into the future face each other. Can they live side by side? Could they interpenetrate? Or must we choose between them?

This book is my effort to gamble on the dance that listens to the past and reconfigures its music to shape a changing future. It is my effort to consider the Hebrew Bible not just a theme awaiting variations, á la Beethoven, but a pattern under transformation by a John Coltrane.

I understand our earthquake as so primal, so all-encompassing, that it comes from the unleashing of the most primal creative energies we know: Creator God, beyond our stories. And I seek to renew and transform the stories that some of us tell about that God: new metaphors, new rules of good behavior and the joy of living in new blessings, new prohibitions on new "sins" fraught with great danger, new symbols and festivals and practices, old ones infused with new significance.

What we thought were sins may as the world keeps dancing become a waltz or a mambo into new blessings. Conversely, habits that we wore without noticing may now seem dangerous and sinful. That's what happens when we dance in the trembling, quaking, dancing, world.

So in each of the chapters that follow, I look at some ancient sins that have taught us new blessings and some ancient sacred practices that now seem sinful. There are several major dimensions of what the Bible sees as making up a sacred community that I will address, as they arise in different forms: the community's relationship with Earth; its relationship with "outsiders" who live in its midst or seek to enter its borders; within the community, relationships between women and men and relationships between the economically or politically powerful and those who were disempowered; and its relationship with the Holy One, especially as understood through God's "Name" and God's "Image."

As we learn how to dance in the earthquake, it is not adequate to say the traditional line: "May I have this dance with you?"

Instead, we say, "May we join this dance together?"

And hear the answer coming with a smile, a riddle in a different language: "May we?—*Mais oui!*—But yes!" For truth only comes when we weave our varied tongues together and laugh to hear the riddle solve itself.

* * *

"I Can't Breathe"—WE Can't Breathe—Earth Can't Breathe

As I write a few days before Juneteenth, an especially poignant celebration of freedom for Black America this year, one of the most amazing Earthquakes in American history is still gaining strength: a multiracial Uprising against systemic racism.

For if the police, who are what makes the state a State—the authority that is entitled to use legitimate violence—act over and over in racist ways, then the society as a whole is crucially compromised.

The last nine minutes of George Floyd's life—in which he said again and again, "I can't breathe"—strike to the heart of us all. We must not permit any State to choke the breath from George Floyd or any other human being or any community of us—race, people, religion, gender.

It is uncanny that the human race as a whole is at this moment struck with a viral disease that attacks most powerfully the ability to breathe.

And uncanny again that at this moment we live as part of a planet that is choking, "We can't breathe." For the age-old exchange of carbon dioxide and oxygen between all vegetation and all animals, including humans—is the Great Breathing that keeps Earth alive. Too much CO2—the "climate crisis"—blocks our breathing.

As I affirm in Chapter 5, the crucial biblical "Name of God"—*YHWH*—is "unpronounceable" because "*YHWH*," with no vowels, is just a Breath.

Every effort to choke the breath from a living person or a community or a species or the planet is a violation of God's Name. We "take the Name in vain" whenever we forget that every breath we take is Itself the Name, and is part of that great Breath that is the Holy One.

1

Healing the Perennial Sin of Eden

Q: "David, how did it feel to wave them [branches of palm, willow, and myrtle along with the lemony etrog] in all the directions of the world]?"

A: David Waskow (age 10): "I felt like I was a tree. I could feel my own branches waving in the wind!"

Are the trees of the field human?

—Deuteronomy 20:19

In our generation, we have invented for ourselves the danger of destroying, at minimum, human civilization and, at maximum, most or all of the web of life on Earth, either with a bang (nuclear holocaust) or a whimper (climate chaos). That sin is at least hanging over the whole world.

In some ways, that sin is being committed by a large proportion of humanity. In other ways, it is committed only by a few—organized to control very large and powerful institutions.

The many who take part are even more forcibly caught than those who kept smoking cigarettes because they were addicted to the nicotine; the carbon burners are compelled by an economic structure that forces everyone to burn fossil fuels. The real culprits were and are the few—the drug lords of tobacco, oil, coal, and unnatural gas.

The warnings of this enormous sin seem to me to go back to the parable of Eden. By "parable" I mean neither fictional fantasy nor factual history; a parable is a teaching story. I think the Eden parable, which locates itself at the dawn of human history, does indeed point to a sin that recurs in many human settlements and many eras.

What is this sin? It is clear to me that what sin we see in the Eden story depends on what struggles we are facing in our selves. Augustine of Hippo was obsessed with the attractions of sex. His sexual nerves were strung so tight as to thrum at the barest touch. He could not bear to be so lured, and so he turned to revulsion. He saw the Bible's vision of the earliest moments of human history through the eyes of that revulsion.

Augustine powerfully affected many leaders of the Christianity of his time. They must have shared much of his tightened strum of tension. Ever since, Christian thought—at least until the Protestant rebellion, and even in some Protestant churches—has suggested that the mistake of Eden was sexual. According to this sexual hysteria, the sin has entered into all future humans because Adam and Eve passed it to their children through intercourse and procreation—like a permanent genetic defect carried not in the genes but by the very act of passing on the genes. Since then, most Christian dogma has seen intense pleasure in the sexual act as not only the bearer of Adam's sin but the nature of the sin itself.

And Augustine's "original" sin was original not only because it was the first, but because it was intimately involved in the origin of the human species and in the origin of every specific human being. It was and is indelibly imprinted in the human condition. It was and is the "sin of all," of the entire world.

Since it infects us all from birth to death, nothing we can do can cancel it. Except one thing, and that comes from outside ourselves, from God. This original sin can be dissolved only through belief in Jesus as the Christ who by coming into the world and submitting to the Crucifixion took all sin upon God's shoulders—and redeemed believers from it.

I should add that through the centuries, some Christian thought—today, a great deal of Christian thought—and most Jewish thought has refused to believe that the sin of Eden—whatever it was—made sex or sexual desire or sexual pleasure in itself sinful, or that the mistake of Adam and Eve delivered that sin into all human souls and bodies.

When Protestantism and Eastern Orthodoxy affirmed that the bearer of spiritual leadership and religious wisdom could be not a single celibate man but a family—a man, a woman, and their children—it was already in body, even if not in words, asserting that sex could live in the heart of religion, not merely in its less serious followers. By insisting on male celibacy for almost all its priests and prelates, the Catholic Church pursued a profoundly different worldview.

The conflict that in the time of the Protestant rebellion seemed to be about other issues seems now, in the context of Modernity, to center on the nature of sexuality and the nature of women. Changes in our answers to those questions have already become some of the major tremors in our worldwide earthquake.

If not sexuality itself, what then was the sin in the Eden parable? If the mistake of Eden was not imposed upon all human beings simply by their birth from sexual conception, what do I mean when I say the mistake of Eden keeps recurring? And how do we turn away from it?

Like and unlike Augustine, I come, of course, with my own bias about what sin it is that threatens all humanity and what blessing of Edenic abundance we instead could choose to share.

I am haunted by the Bomb and the Climate Crisis, and at the same time inspired by the vision of an ecologically delightful planet. Perhaps my own understanding of the sin of Eden comes partly from the deep imprint still on me of 1968, of seeing Pharaoh in our own generation, and of the joyful alternative if we could only cross the Red Sea into the Promised Land, the milk-and-honey Garden.

Indeed, it is precisely contemplating the possible death of human civilization and the torment that would mean for my grandchildren that brings me to look at the birth of humankind and at this powerful mythic parable of our beginning.

To understand the parable of Eden, we must begin just before Eden. The Bible says, "No shrub of the field was yet on the earth . . . *because* there was no human to till the soil" (Genesis 2:5). This suggests that the reason for the Creator to birth the human race is the need for shrubs and grasses to have the loving touch of human presence—an early wisdom about the intertwining of what we would now call an ecosystem. The shrubs need us to grow them; we need them to feed us or in meadows to feed the goats and sheep who fed us. It is a farmer's vision, a shepherd's vision.

(Notice that it is part of the Bible's second Creation story. The first one, with its practically liturgical recitation of three pairs of days surmounted by Shabbat, was written by priests whose chief concern was liturgy. In ancient Israel, priests were not farmers. We see the power of the hot concerns of those who shaped not only interpretation of the sacred text but the text itself.)

The intertwining of reddish soil and human farmer goes so deep that there is indeed a birthing. From the *adamah* (earth) comes forth *adam* (the human earthling). First this newborn loses the *-ah*, the Hebrew letter *hei* that is the sound of breathing. Then *YHWH Elohim*, "Breath of Life Creator God blew into the newborn's nostrils the breath of life, and the human became a living, breathing person" (Genesis 2:5–7). (Why do I translate "*YHWH*" as "Breath of Life"? Because if you try to pronounce that Name of God as the letters of the Name indicate, without any vowels, what you are likely to hear and feel is *YyyyHhhhWwwwHhhh*, the sound not of silence but of breathing. For a fuller exploration of this Name, see Chapter 5.)

This tale of birthing humankind was itself born from the birthing of an individual human being. While the fetus is still in the mother's womb, it has no independent breath. The mother's breathing sustains it through the placenta. This mother–child interweave is like the adamah. When the newborn loses this organic, suffused breath—this -ah, this letter hei—it must take its first independent breath. Perhaps someone taps the newborn's rear end—in Yiddish, their *tush*—or breathes into its mouth, or nose. The child begins to breathe.

This biological process is the very model for the Torah's story of how adam is born from adamah—from Mother Earth. Since the mother here is not a mammal but the earth itself, which sprouts the shrubs and trees as the soil sprouts humankind, we see another artful teaching reinforcing that Earth and earthling, the humus and humanity, are family.

YyyyHhhhWwwwHhhh, the Breath of Life, shapes a lump of reddish clay—adamah in Hebrew—into an androgynous human form. Then in "Eden," which means "Delight," *YHWH* speaks to the human race: "On this Earth there is wonderful abundance. Eat of it in joy. But you must restrain yourselves just a little: Of this one tree, don't eat" (Genesis 2:15–17).

But the tree is delightful to see and delicious to eat. So the human species refuses to restrain itself, eats from the forbidden tree, and as a result the abundance disappears. Only by toiling every day of our lives, the story warns us, with the sweat pouring down our faces, will we find enough to eat from an Earth that gives forth mostly thorns and thistles (Genesis 2:17–19).

This sin is indeed perennial. Over and over, humankind has overreached to gobble up a piece of the Earth from which we gain our sustenance. And, by overreaching, has brought it into ruin. In our own lives, we relived this "first" disaster in the Gulf of Mexico, during the summer of 2010. The Big Oil corporation BP would not restrain itself, and the result was the death of its own workers and disastrous damage to the overflowing abundance of the Gulf.

This was not a moment unique in human history: The cautionary tale of the ruined Garden of Delight has been ignored by many human cultures that have despoiled some sacred patch of Earth. It has become indeed not an "original" sin but a perennial sin.

Was the sin avoidable? If we look back at the Eden parable from a different angle, we may see it as a tale of growing up. The newborn humankind, breathing on its own, becomes an infant: fed without lifting a finger, naked without feeling shame or desire, bounded by the gentlest of boundaries, warned of an apocalyptic ending if it breaks the boundary.

Yet Humanity grows up another stage, by meeting the "Snake": a being still more naked than we are—more naked than all the other beasts of the field—because it sheds even its own skin—and survives! The Snake then goes to Eve. Perhaps he says to her, "I shed my own skin—and do not die, but grow and transform myself. You too, unlike your friend Adam, shed your skin each month. And when you do, you bleed. Your blood may seem to be your death—but like me, you survive transformed! Do not believe this edict. Push comes to shove, the One Who is the Breath of Life will breathe new life into you; you will not die."[1]

Eve saw the Tree; it looked delightful. It smelled delicious. She could not bear to live an ascetic life of self-denial. Babyhood is boring, and babyhood forever even worse. How could self-transformation be an error? Adam might not understand, for he could not shed his skin and keep on living.

Would she rebel, grow one step into a rebellious adolescence? She would. She did. She ate. And she persuaded Adam it was time for transformation.

An instant consequence of adolescence: nakedness became both alluring and alarming.

And the Snake was partly right. The human race did not die out, despite its spoliation of the Garden. It was indeed transformed. But at what cost! For adolescence lasted but a moment. The next stage of their life, our lives, was an adulthood of drudgery, shame, subjugation, and conflict.

Why? Because we had broken a rule much more important than we guessed. Not an arbitrary rule imposed by an imperious parent, but a violation of reality that forces a deeper level of reality into operation: What we sow is what we reap. Bending the Earth to our will forces the Earth to bend us to its will.

---

[1] This is an unconventional view of the role of the Snake. It is rooted in my view of the use of the Hebrew word "*arum*" in the text. First the Bible says that Adam and Eve were "*arumim*"—"naked," in the plural. Then in the very next verse it says that the Snake was the "most *arum*" of all the beasts of the field. All translators assume that this second "*arum*" comes from a different Hebrew root that means something entirely different—"clever," or "shrewd." I think the writer who juxtaposed these two "*arum*" words knew exactly what he was doing—and meant the Snake was even more naked than all other unclothed animals because of being able to shed its skin without dying. Perhaps the author reveled in the double meaning of *arum*: that the Snake was also cleverer than other animals because it knew this truth—that it could transform itself without dying.

So the Garden's abundance disappears. We enter an adulthood of drudgery: Hard work to make a living as the Earth turns sullen. Hard work to be a parent when our children quarrel, when the elder insists he is entitled to supremacy and strikes a deadly blow when the younger, weaker, gentler supersedes him.

We should not ignore the fact that the parable uses the imagery of parents and children to instruct us. And we should also not ignore the truth that it is how *we* conceive our relationship with the Earth, how we understand the "rules" that come from inside Reality, not imposed from somewhere outside, that shape how we act.

Surely "growing up" was not itself a sin. But the way we chose to grow up was through an act of subjugation of our Mother Earth, a decision to gobble up all the abundance while ignoring the warnings that sprang from our own decent sense of our own Reality. The choice to grow up did not need to be sinful. But that particular choice of *how* to grow up was sinful. Could we instead have chosen to go beyond our Parent by a greater overflowing of unbounded love?

Or to put it in a different way, could we have conceived of a form of self-restraint that could have protected the Earth from subjugation while feeling attractive to us, not repellent? Is there a way to grow beyond endless drudgery, and also beyond the impulse to subjugate, to a wiser elderhood? An elderhood that chooses technology and a social system that relieves us all from drudgery without subjugating and shattering the Earth? Today that question is the hinge of human history.

Today we are faced with the prospect that if we cannot learn to restrain ourselves from pouring CO_2 and methane into the atmosphere of Earth, the sacred Interbreathing of all life, we will ruin the abundance of the planet as a whole. And indeed the warning of Eden could become a truth: our arrogance toward the Earth could bring about our death.

The Hebrew Scriptures do point us toward another path—toward growing up into maturity. The Bible does offer us, in another parable, a different way of imagining and exercising self-restraint. It tells this parable after telling the story of a "concentration of arrogance"—as if first to make us face the worst danger before offering us a humane way out.

First the Bible tells the long and painful tale of the Pharaoh whose arrogance, stubbornness, and cruelty bring slavery upon his people and ecodisastrous Plagues upon his country. This story brings the basic teaching of the Garden parable much closer to the living realities we face. For in it, we can recognize politicians and rulers whom we know: rulers whose arrogance toward human beings bubbles over into arrogance that wrecks the very earth that nurtures their peoples and themselves. We learn how the cruelty of such a ruler brings about his own death and the dissolution of his power in the Red Sea. It is as if we need a "real-life" history to give skin and flesh to the bare-bones parable of Eden.

But the Torah is not satisfied to tell us only tales of tragedy and overreach. We need to learn from carrots to feed us, not only from sticks to beat us. So after Pharaoh, the Torah tells us another parable, a story that points toward the healing of the disaster at the end of Eden.

This is the parable of *Manna* and Shabbat (Exodus 16). For now the universe showers us again with almost free abundance. The only work we need to do is to walk forth every morning and gather the Manna—a strange "vegetation" that is like coriander seed but far more nourishing.

No sweat, no toil, no thorns and thistles. Self-restraint is built in: anyone who tries to gather more than enough to eat for a day finds that the extra rots and stinks. On the sixth day, enough Manna falls to feed the people for another day; and it does not rot. It will meet their needs for the seventh day. On the seventh day, Shabbat, no Manna falls. No point in trying to gather it. Self-restraint is again built in.

But this is a different kind of self-restraint. In Eden, self-restraint meant giving up a portion of delight. The tree was beautiful; its aroma beckoned toward a delicious taste. Who could embrace asceticism in the face of such a tree?

But Shabbat is a kind of self-restraint that itself is filled with joy and celebration. This is a new invention, and it beckons toward a way of relating with the Earth that is filled with love, not domination, and gives a fuller life to both adam and adamah.

If the coming of Shabbat into human awareness and action is in this parable, the way forth from the tragedy of Eden, then it might be said that in Jewish theology Shabbat—the new Eden and the foretaste of the Messianic Age—is analogous to the "new Adam"—Christ—in Christian thought. For Jews, it is observing Shabbat that can save us from this perennial sin. For Christians, it is living a life of nonviolence and compassion, walking the path as Jesus walked it, that can bring the days of peace and justice.

The point of a parable is teaching us how to behave in real-life history. How do we turn this parable into an active practice when we leave the Magical Space of Wilderness and cross the river into becoming shepherds and farmers?

The Bible answers this question with the teaching of the great *Shabbat Shabbaton*, the *Shmita* year when (Leviticus 25:1–7) we must celebrate a year-long Shabbat, when we must restrain ourselves from organizing the sowing and the reaping that are the necessities of ordinary agriculture.

Not only that. The fences between "my" land and "your" land are knocked down for a year. Not only people but domesticated animals and wild beasts may glean freely whatever freely grows, without an organized harvesting. "For the land is Mine!" says *YHWH*, the Interbreathing Spirit of all life. "You are only sojourners, visiting residents, with Me."

And Deuteronomy, probably reflecting real social crises in the history of the Israelite kingdoms, adds to this year of restful peace with Earth that this year will also embody a restful peace between the rich and the poor. For in this same year, debtors will have their debts annulled. The anxiety, fear, and resentment that rise from owing money, the anxiety, fear, and contempt that arise from needing to collect it, are annulled.

This year-long Shabbat, like the weekly one-day Pausing, is not ascetic; keeping it will bring more joy, not less and more abundance, not less. If we fail to let the Earth keep this Shabbat, reality will bring down on our heads a lethal "restfulness." Indeed, the Torah sarcastically says the Earth will "rest"—live the Shabbats it has been denied—through drought, famine, floods, plague, and exile (see Leviticus 26, esp. 14–46, and 2 Chronicles 36:20–21).

The disasters listed in Leviticus 26 are echoed today in the predictions of climate scientists who warn us of the consequences of overworking Earth by burning fossil fuels—choking its air, its Breath. The Shmita came often enough to let Earth rebalance itself as human intervention paused. The warnings, from ancient Bible and from modern science, speak from the fear or the fact that a number of Sabbatical/Shmita years have not been allowed to happen. In our own generation, we can count about fifty Shmita years (since the beginning of the Industrial Revolution) that we have not allowed to happen. The pent-up need to rest has become explosive. What can we learn from this ancient teaching about what we need to do?

The first answer of climate scientists to this question was that what we need to do is rapidly to reduce and swiftly to eliminate the burning of all carbon fuels and to replace them with renewable energy that comes from sun and wind. More recently, increasing numbers of scientists are warning that even achieving zero CO_2 emissions will leave a trillion tons of excess carbon dioxide in the atmosphere. That can wreak havoc on, and possibly even destroy, human civilization. To heal our planet will require getting that lethal CO_2 out of the atmosphere, or otherwise canceling its effect.

The ancient rabbis taught that it takes three pillars to keep the world upright. Today we need to erect three pillars to prevent climate chaos and catastrophe:

1. We need to continue and swiftly increase our work to achieve zero CO_2 emissions.
2. To heal our planet will require getting the lethal overload of CO_2 out of the atmosphere, or otherwise canceling its effect. *So we need to take new steps to renew and restore a healthy, life-giving planet: an Earth, a planet, as life giving for our children and grandchildren as it was for our parents and grandparents.*
3. We need to create communities that are culturally, economically, and politically "resilient"—that can come back from experiencing some of the storms, wildfires, epidemics, and so on, that are bound to afflict us before we can restore our grandparents' climate.

We already know how to shape the first pillar. We need to end the burning of all fossil fuels, including unnatural gas. (If you have to smash rocks with tons of chemicalized water pressure to get burnable gas out of them, that gas ain't "natural.") We need to protect the remaining great forests and restore millions of deforested acres to grow CO_2-absorbing trees. We need to replace great herds of methane-emitting cattle with other forms of protein. Since our thirst for energy swells each year, each decade, we need to make even cheaper and more efficient the technology of solar and wind renewable energy. Can we do all these? There are three problems that we face in doing them.

One is that huge and profitable institutions have grown up, these two hundred years or so, that make their money by burning fossil fuels. They spend a small proportion of their Hyperwealth on buying politicians, scientists, and journalists to lie about the fact that their Hyperprofits are burning not just coal and oil but Planet Earth. Global scorching, not global "warming." They have become as addicted to their own wealth and power as the ancient biblical Pharaoh—and like him, they enslave human beings and bring plagues upon the Earth. How do we dissolve their power in the nearest Sea of Reeds?

The second problem is the fixation on the Carbon Economy from those whose livelihoods are hanging onto it by their fingernails—coal miners, oil refinery workers, the towns and small businesses that depend on their meager incomes. They are hooked on Carbon not because they make so much money from it but because the little they do make comes only from it. They see the shaky handwriting on the Earthquake's planetary wall, but that stirs many of them not to transformation but to a desperate clinging to the past, even a desperate fury at those who welcome transformation. In God's Earthquake, they seek to hang on to the "immovable" past. They are not wrong to be frightened. The only decent answer to their fear and despair is to make sure that "social justice" and "ecological sanity" go together. Just as the Shmita/Sabbatical Year merged the two, so a modern version of it must. The Carbon workers must be invited into the Dance with new jobs at good pay—jobs to emplace the Renewable Economy. The Shmita welcomed everyone into the sharing process: servants and foreigners as well as landholders and the homeborn. All could eat from the freely growing produce of an uncoerced Earth; all could eat from what was stored up ahead of time as the Shmita year approached. And in every Shmita year, according to Deuteronomy 15:1–3, all debts were to be annulled. Just as Earth and its farmers are released from their work, so all Israelites are released from their debts. The healing of adamah must come and not at the cost of oppressing adam.

The third problem is that when we meet "the enemy," many of them turn out to be us. It is the same problem that the Humans faced in Eden. Can we bear to restrain ourselves, to give up even a few of our pleasures for the sake of Life? And the answer must be learned from the parable of Manna and Shabbat. We must create forms of self-restraint that are celebratory, delightful, filled with the pleasures of the Manna that tasted like whatever flavors we desired. Filled with the singing, the loving, the dancing of Shabbat.

The first two problems require wrenching national political decisions in many countries, the United States among them. Decisions about public taxes, public grants, public investments. The third problem requires grassroots action. It requires the creation of face-to-face groups that can turn self-restraint into pleasure and can turn local communities into agents of national change.

The first two problems also require not only national decisions but locally rooted demands. Otherwise, national change will not happen. The opposition arrayed against it, from the Hyperwealthy Carbon Pharaohs to the desperate Carbon workers, cannot be overcome without local communities that resist Carbon pipelines and create new energy sources. It is no accident that the biblical call for a fiftieth year of Jubilee Home Bringing (crowning the seventh-year rhythm with a seven-times-seven-plus-one rhythm) requires that every family be able to return to its ancestral plot of land. The local unit must be strengthened for the national transformation to be done.

How might we bring about this way of Dancing in the Earthquake? Let's start at the local level. There have already been numerous cases of local resistance to pipelines that would carry Carbon fuels across regions and nations. Not only do these pipelines endanger great round Earth, they poison neighborhoods and regions with asthma and cancer, undrinkable water, and unbreathable air. Perhaps the most famous case of this kind of resistance was at Standing Rock in the Dakotas, where Native communities resisted an oil pipeline that endangered their sacred burial grounds and drinking water—indeed, the water of millions who drink from the Missouri River. They did not resist alone: as the call of Spirit and of "Water is life!" reached beyond the tribal dances and vigils, thousands of others came to stand at Standing Rock. The spiritual grounding of the indigenous resistance called to heart and soul. Now there are many such resistance centers, some directly against regional pipelines and some against the official regulatory commissions that have till recently blithely given any permits that Carbon companies commanded.

The creative cousins of these movements to resist old Carbon have been the neighborly creation of wind or solar co-ops. They represent a classic form of social change: creating in the present a social form that we imagine for the future. The sit-ins were a classic model: if we imagine in the future a nation full of racially integrated drug stores and restaurants, begin by simply integrating a few and raising a flag for emulation. In the same vein, closer to the heart of power, if the goal is equal voting rights for all in a state where Blacks are not allowed to vote, hold an unofficial election where everyone can vote, and challenge the established official bodies to recognize as real the officials so elected. That is what the Mississippi Freedom Democratic Party did in 1964. The results included some murdered activists, a national hearing, and a temporary defeat that helped to spark a movement that brought about the Voting Rights Act of 1965. After almost fifty years of fruitful political change, the Act was gutted by a backlash Supreme Court. The struggle continues.

Creating solar co-ops threatens electrical utilities and the "regulators" they control, and the Carbon corporations have tried to contain the process; but so far, there have been no murders. What began as a single solar co-op in a neighborhood of Washington, DC, has becomes a swarm across the city and then new hubs of solar co-ops in spots around the country.

There are different ways for most households to choose to light their homes with wind or solar power. They may fit into different lifestyles lived by those who make the choice. One is by signing on to a wind-power or solar-energy company, just as anonymous and distant as the companies that deliver electricity from coal. The connection is purely financial. It matters to Earth but not very much to people. A second is by organizing a local co-op that is purely a business, bound by money and by intricate engineering. "Get the job done!" is the organizational mandate. The third is by creating solar co-ops at the neighborhood or congregational level. The co-ops operate on a face-to-face basis. Not only would its members share the struggles to choose a solar installer and meet the needs of each other for advice and perhaps for loans; they would meet each other. They would physically meet and spiritually "meet": meet perhaps once a month to dance, tell stories, sing about moments of success or disappointment; share food and cook together; plan the politics of challenging a major corporation or a government official. (A co-op is a business. It's allowed.) If we are taking the Manna/Shabbat parable as wise teaching, then where possible, this would be the best alternative. It would take the co-op members more time; but the time it would take would be "time out," the joys of Sabbath.

A second hands-on possibility is to take your car—as the saying goes—please! As the prices for electric cars keep dropping and the availability of charging stations grows, you can buy your own. You could arrange car-pooling that will be enjoyable. Even better, check to see whether there's a neighborly group that would like to ride a commuter train together. (I know one such group of Amtrak passengers that stayed together on their New York–North Philadelphia journey for more than thirty years. They helped each other through emergencies, celebrated birthdays, mourned a death. When a member left, they threw a farewell party and gave her a model railroad car, signed by them all, as a memento.) "Giving up" the car became a pleasure, not a deprivation.

Reducing CO_2 emissions as a communal joy, not an individual duty, will often help to shape the third pillar, resilience. For example, solarized neighborhoods cannot only reduce CO_2 emissions but can also come back much faster if the central electricity grid goes down from a hyperhurricane, as happened in Puerto Rico recently.

And doing solarization through neighborhood and congregational co-ops will build cultural and political resilience, too. The local utility or a governmental agency tries to block solarization? The co-op can work together to stymie their opposition. And that political work can be infused with song, with meals together, with sharing recipes. If disaster strikes, people who care about each other will come out of their trauma more easily.

To deal with the second pillar—restoring a healthy climate, healing the wounded Earth beyond a fever pill or a Band-Aid—we need much more study. Both technological and religious/spiritual/ethical study. Clergyfolk and scientists should get together. A rabbi and an oceanographer must walk into a bar together. And a church. And a seminar room.

Various proposals are being put forward to get this excess carbon dioxide out of the atmosphere or to take even more radical steps that might reverse Earth's overheating. Some of the proposed steps could be swift, effective, and very risky. Others could be slower, less certain, and safer. Which do we choose?

What should be the relationships among religion, science, and public policy in addressing this crisis? What are these proposals, what are their risks and possibilities? What do the various Bibles of our varied wisdom traditions teach about the roots of the climate crisis: not only how we should behave toward the Earth but also how to balance the risks of action and of inaction, how to judge among the various proposed solutions, and how to engage (through study, liturgy, daily practice, and advocacy) the varied religious communities in making these decisions?

Shmita is the Torah's effort to teach us a path of practical peace in the human community and between the Earth and human earthlings. Transforming even a pastoral/agricultural society for just a year was not so easy. How can we translate that pattern into our lives today, much more intricately intertwined?

All right, let's try imagining. Please keep in mind that these are simply imaginings, intended to stretch our minds. The basic goal is to accomplish two changes: to weaken the power of institutions that are burning the Earth for their own profit and to strengthen grassroots communities in their ability and desire to use renewable energy.

Perhaps under modern conditions and the urgency of planetary crisis, the seven-year pattern does not fit our needs. Or perhaps we can imagine ways in which the rhythm still might.

Perhaps federal subsidies go to fund local neighborhood groups to create the kind of neighborhood solar or wind-energy co-ops that I have mentioned. They aim to make turning away from fossil fuels not an act of ascetic self-denial but an enjoyable communal celebration. The same co-ops also receive subsidies to hold week-long neighborhood festivals during the year—sports, music, poetry, art, dance, cookery, storytelling. During those weeks, nonresidents of the neighborhood may drive only wind- or solar-driven electric vehicles into the festival neighborhoods, and residents are asked to leave gasoline-driven cars unmoving for the week. They use shoes and bikes and electric golf carts to get around. Again, joy rather than resentment accompanies the shift to a sustainable society. And grant support at the neighborhood level encourages the flowering and honoring of many local cultures in affirmation, not annoyance, with each other. No one needs to feel like a "forgotten" American.

Perhaps a broad range of religious organizations announce that "Only Grass-Fed Beef and Milk Is Kosher!" They will no longer use beef or drink milk in any communal celebrations, unless it comes from certifiably grass-fed cows, and they urge their members, congregants, and everyone to stop eating other beef or drinking other milk. Why? (1) Herds of cattle fed on grain in feedlots, rather than on grass in open fields, produce large amounts of methane, which is many times as powerful a planet-heating gas as CO_2. Though methane lasts for a much shorter time in the atmosphere than CO_2, its potency and the constant pouring of more of it into the air as consumption of beef and milk increases make it an important danger that can be averted by citizen action, followed up by new legislation or corporate agreement. (2) Many cattle-raising businesses destroy forests that absorb CO_2 and turn it into oxygen, in order to turn the slashed forest land into feedlots for cattle. Insisting on raising grass-fed cattle radically reduces these dangers. What might begin as multireligious buying clubs could spread, as did the demand for organic produce—once a tiny niche, now a major item in many grocery chains. This action would emulate the ancient rabbis who forbade raising goats and sheep in the Land of Israel, even though the Abrahamic clan did precisely that. The rabbis acted because, as the numbers of sheep and goats grew ever greater, they were destroying meadowland. Chicken and fish do not produce methane, and both provide the protein necessary to many humans. People could gather for celebrations of becoming committed practitioners of "New Kosher," thus providing the sense of joyful comradeship that, as we have seen, can support a kind of self-restraint that is not self-denial.

Perhaps, in memory of the Shmita/Sabbatical Year but not locked into just one year of restorative action, there begins a massive reforestation campaign all over the world, including the planting of millions of trees in cities and suburbs. This effort could recapture millions of tons of CO_2 from the atmosphere. The tree planting becomes a time of celebration—song, food, storytelling—in every community.

Perhaps, to embody the Shmita/Sabbatical Year, we apply a 10 percent surtax on the average annual income and on the accumulated wealth of all people and corporations with ten million or more dollars average yearly income in the previous six years, or one billion dollars in accumulated wealth. The money collected goes into a Climate Healing Fund to support workers in carbon industries to shift their work and their lives, to support low-income Americans in switching to renewable energy sources, and to support low-income nations for the same purpose. Such a tax would probably face fierce opposition from entrenched Hyperwealthy people and Carbon-Pharaoh corporations. At the same time, it would benefit local grassroots communities and might therefore create its own constituency of support. So, organizing for this effort would need to go forward during the six years before every Shmita year.[2]

---

[2] When I wrote the paragraph above, it seemed an almost impossible political stretch to make such a program into real-life national policy. But only six months later, a group of young people utterly changed the political dynamic by taking their own futures seriously. Not only as an intellectual construct but as a visceral reality, they knew, felt, grokked that their lives are on the line. They know that if they are eighteen or twenty-two now, by the time they are forty or fifty years old, they will be front-line victims, suffering famines, fires, and diseases brought on by the Carbon system. So they decided to act. Sitting in at Speaker Pelosi's office, talking back to a dismissive Senator Feinstein, stopping traffic for a week in downtown London, they caught the attention and fired up the smoldering commitment of their peers and their elders.

They put forth the Green New Deal of knitting together the urgent social and economic need for millions of well-paying new jobs with the urgent planetary and neighborly need to move beyond the Carbon system.

Perhaps, just perhaps, you can imagine your own "perhaps." Talk with your neighbors, friends, and co-workers to improve it, and then act upon it. The proposals I have just sketched are simply efforts to imagine practical ways of making real change. Do these provisions sufficiently reward the pleasures of self-restraint and communal decision-making? Do they lead the way toward a broader culture of interconnection with all life? That is the test by which they should be measured, and the specific practices suggested here are only speculations, imaginations, to stir the juices of experiment along the way.

The Shmita year is the fullest envisioning in our sacred writings of ecopractice—practical life in the embodiment of peaceful interconnection. And then the sacred texts reach once more beyond the practical, to lift up a vision of that peace made whole. In the Song of Songs, we see and hear and smell and taste the Garden for grown-ups—Eden for a grown-up human race.

In the Song, Earth is playful, joyful, freely giving forth the nuts and fruits of Eden. We humans have learned to love the Earth, not subjugate it.

And in the Song, the second disaster of Eden has been healed as well. In the Song that is beyond all songs, no longer do men rule over women. In the next chapter, we seek to dance in the earthquake that comes with this transformation.

And within weeks, they had won support for the Green New Deal from serious candidates for president and hundreds of members of Congress. I think the Green New Deal is the nearest analogue for a modern society of what the Sabbatical/Shmita was for biblical society. The campaign for it has heartened me to keep putting forward "imaginary" possibilities that now seem fantasies but need only committed unconventional action to enter the realm of real political possibilities.

2

The World beyond Subjugating Women

One way of looking at the Eden story is that it is a Just-So story in the Kipling tradition: In our world, snakes crawl on their bellies. Why? In our world, men work very hard in order to provide our families with the food we eat. Why? In our world, men are in charge and women do what they say. Why? But these Just-So stories are not just whimsical. The answers to "Why?" become a parable, a teaching story, like so.

The Just-So story (Genesis 2 and 3) that answers why the Snake must crawl starts just before the Snake's invitation to Eve. As we have already seen, perhaps the Snake was arum, naked, because it could shed its skin, and arum, shrewd, because it knew that doing this meant it could transform itself without dying—and knew that Eve could also shed her skin through menstruation, transform herself, without dying.

Did the Snake speak to Eve rather than Adam because the Snake knew that as a woman, once a month she shed her own skin, bled, but did not die? If the Eden story is a story of the stages through which the human race grows up, transforming itself, letting an old self die so that a new self could live, then Eve, precisely because she is a woman, is the hero of the story.

But Eve suffers consequences precisely in her womanness for her sin—her part in refusing to restrain herself from gobbling up the fruit of the fragrant tree. She will have pain in the labor of giving birth. She will have desire for her man, but he will rule over her.

What if the consequence named in the story, that the Snake must crawl on his belly and eat dust—is the consequence not for its invitation to Eve to transcend herself but a warning that in an effort to transform ourselves we must seek compassion for, not conquest over, the Earth and all Creation?

Why? What went wrong? The Just-So story tells us that the Snake and the human race had overmastered the Earth, reduced it to an object. The result? What you sow is what you reap. Not punishment, but rather a consequence.

The Snake encouraged the human race to subjugate the Earth, our mother. The consequence is that the Snake itself is subjugated. Instead of eating from the delicious Tree, it will swallow only dust. "What you sow is what you reap."

Adam would not restrain himself from subjugating Earth's abundance, and as a consequence, he is subjugated to the Earth's refusal of abundance. "What you sow is what you reap."

Eve decides to subjugate Mother Earth by eating from the Tree. She and human motherhood are subjugated. She uses Adam's desire to please her to persuade him to eat. So she must be subjugated to her desire to please her man. Where she had ruled over him, he will rule over her. "What you sow is what you reap."

What if the story had told us that the Snake said to Eve:

> For you to grow up, you must listen to every teaching that the Breath of Life whispers in your ear, and then you can choose to do something different! Create a new life of your own! If you heard the Interbreathing Spirit tell you not to touch the Tree, suppose you drape a garland of

> flowers on the tree and dance around it. Invite your friend Adam to dance with you. Touch the tree, sing to the tree, climb the Tree, *make the Tree your friend.*
>
> No need to eat its fruit—for eating would make the Tree your tool, your instrument, and not your friend. You will learn something new when you do this dance, and you will become like me—for your skin will shed like mine and you will be transformed, like me. Your friend the Tree will become the Tree of Life Ever-Growing, and you will never die.

And then, what if the story had ended in the following way?

> And the Breath of Life said to Eve, "Your impulse was so creative, so life-giving, and your invitation to Adam so joyful, that you and he will walk into the world as a Garden of Delight, side by side and equal by equal. Your desire for each other shall suffuse your children and future generations with love for each other."

How pleasant! How joyful! Why could we not have a story like that to start history?

Because that was not the world the writers of the story lived in. In their world, people died. In their world, food was scarce, and men worked hard to grow it. In their world, men ruled and women obeyed.

But the storytellers did not think that people were stuck in this story forever. Indeed, they told the story this way precisely to teach people not to subjugate Earth. The Bible intends to teach the human race to grow up, to keep growing up, beyond an adulthood of drudgery and beyond an adulthood where men rule over women.

Let me be clear: That is the world vision that beckons and beacons to me. That is what I seek to find in the sacred text, not only because finding it would make me more comfortable with its sacredness but also because I want to understand how to get to that world. And I imagine that these teachings, centuries old, might have some wisdom about how to keep growing up.

Let us start with the messages from the Breath of Life/God to Eve and to Adam at the end of the Eden story.

To Eve, the Voice announces that her labor in giving birth will be painful and that her desire will be toward her husband; yet he will rule over her. She has asserted her dominion over this tree that has been reserved from exploitation as if it were a Planetary Park. The consequence of her sin is that women will be dominated by their husbands. But for millennia, our traditions have cited the Eden story as if this subjugation were a command to be obeyed, not a consequence to be transcended: a dismal consequence to be transcended by correcting our mistake in our choice of how to grow up.

Indeed, most of Christian and Jewish thought about women until the last generation has treated this subjugation of women as a duty, responding to the "command" that "He [the male] shall rule over you [the female]." But "He shall rule over you" is no more a "command" than is "You will work with the sweat pouring down your face, yet the Earth will bring forth only thorns and thistles."

To Adam, the Voice says that only through painful labor (the same words as used toward Eve but for him meant in bringing forth food rather than bringing forth children) and through the sweat pouring down his face will he be able to wring food from the earth, which will bring forth mostly thorns and thistles.

No tradition has seen this consequence to Adam as a command to be obeyed. No one, for example, says we are forbidden to ease our labor by using tools to grow our food: a rake, a hoe, a huge metallic harvester. No one suggests that we must not artfully encourage the Earth to be more fruitful than giving forth just thorns and thistles.

Indeed, just the opposite is true; much of human history (including the history of those communities influenced by the Bible) has been devoted to creating tools and techniques to ease labor and make the Earth more fruitful. Why has no one urged that the human race, or its males, should refrain from making and using tools to ease our labor and produce more abundance? Because we knew the prediction was not a command.

"We" knew? Who knew? The men who did indeed rule the roost, those human roosters, did not intend to "obey" a "command" to live their lives in drudgery. They brought their wits to changing history, learning from the Just-So story they began with but not thinking it chained them to its consequences.

But they seem to have had few problems with the Just-So story's description of the subordinate role their wives, their sisters, their daughters, even their mothers would have to play.

Yet read aright, it seems to me, the Bible implores us to keep growing.

Yes, the Just-So aspect of the Eden story recognizes that in the world of the writer, women were subordinate. But just as the Bible is not prohibiting us from creating the tools of greater productivity, greater fruitfulness, just so it is not prohibiting us from seeking to create a world in which women will no longer be subordinate. In fact, it wants us to mature ourselves into that world beyond locked hierarchies.

How do I say this against all the evidence that women are far less visible than men in many biblical stories, that they are usually portrayed as objects rather than creative subjects of events and history, that their strength is usually restricted to their sexuality and their bearing of men's babies? All that is true. But scattered through the Hebrew Bible, in bits and pieces here and there, are stories of women who are not subordinate and whom the Bible honors.

Perhaps most powerful is the story of how two sets of women begin the process of overthrowing the cruel and arrogant power of Pharaoh. The first set, two midwives named Shifra and Puah, are ordered by Pharaoh to kill all the newborn Israelite boys. They refuse and mollify Pharaoh with a pun: They tell him that the Israelite women are so "lively" or so "animated" that they give birth before the midwives can arrive. But he hears that the mothers are like "wildlife" or like "animals." To Pharaoh's racist prejudices, this makes perfect sense. So he commands everyone, not just midwives, to drown the newborns in the Nile (Exodus 1:15–22).

The midwives' action is the first stage of nonviolent resistance—noncooperation. Soon there follows the second stage, led again by women (Exodus 2:1–10). The mother (Yocheved) and sister (Miriam) of a newborn Moses conspire with—of all people—Pharaoh's own daughter. Together they become an "international feminist conspiracy." Together they take active steps to save the newborn's life from Pharaoh's genocidal order. According to the ancient rabbis, the daughter, known only as *Bat Pharaoh*—"Daughter of Pharaoh"—is renamed "*Bat Yah*—"Daughter of the God Who Is the Breath of Life."

The three women who saved the baby Moses drew him forth from a second womb, the river. Moses grows up to become the great leader of the Exodus. But as he journeys from his shepherd's life in Midian to meet his destiny in the Narrowdom of Egypt, his life comes once more into jeopardy. A cryptic story (Exodus 4:24–26) tells us that in his long sojourn away from both his peoples in the Narrow Land, he seems to have overlooked circumcising his son Gershom, or perhaps himself. He is in danger of being swallowed up by an awesome, dangerous God. It is his Midianite wife Tzipporah who realizes the danger, wields a flint of circumcision to make a "bridegroom of blood," and saves his life. So the story makes clear that it took these six women to make the liberation movement possible.

There is a clever *sub rosa* teaching in this story. The subordination of women that the Bible seems to affirm is defined by isolating them into the roles of wife and mother—procreation. Yet here these tales of rebellion turn exactly on the subversive use of those roles. Midwives are a kind of motherhood to the exponential power. They make birth possible for hundreds or thousands of children, many more than any single mother. (And, we should notice, often greatly reducing the pain of childbirth labor. Does the Bible chastise these midwives for violating the "command" that women's pain in labor will be multiplied? Not at all; God rewards them.)

For the Bible, it is exactly when a tyrant subjugates his people, enslaves a community of immigrants, and bring plagues upon the Earth—an ultimate destructive version of the mistake of Eden—that women bring birth giving and compassion to resist. These women give birth not only to Moses but to a whole new community—even a new kind of community, one that teaches the experience of enslavement as precisely the reason for empowered former slaves to treat landless, marginal foreigners with love and justice.

Notice that the story teaches that tyranny brings transformation into becoming. Even though the biblical Exodus is unlikely to be factual history, it may well be a kind of historical novel that draws on memories of campfire songs and stories to enrich and magnify those legends into the iconic epic of a people (and, through borrowing and remembering, more peoples than one). That teaching, a kind of social psychology of tyranny and transformation, has other history to back it up. The history we know as factual suggests the same process.

As we have already seen, it was the tyranny of the Babylonian Empire that destroyed the early Temple and the social system that had been built upon it—in the social equivalent of an earthquake. By doing that, Babylon gave an unintended birth to a burst of creativity among the exiles it dragged off to the Captivity. They crystallized what we know as the Torah and the Prophets.

And it was the tyranny of Rome that, by shattering the Second Temple stage of biblical Judaism, ultimately called into being two new and different kinds of community, Rabbinic Judaism and Christianity. It was the tyranny of the power elite of Mecca that made Mohammed ready to receive new revelation and prepared a society to follow.

And today, we are in the midst of struggle, as Modernity run amok shatters not only all the older cultures and communities but much of the organic fabric of the Earth. It is our struggle that will decide whether new forms of community can emerge and survive: Communities that see the boundaries between themselves not as walls or fences, but as fringes. Communities that see other-than-human species as vital to us, part of "us," wrapping us in a larger community that hovers on the fringe of being One. Communities that embody our new intellectual understanding of the interwovenness of all human cultures and all life-forms. "Ecology" as policy, not merely science.

As we have noticed in the stories of the Exodus, the assignment of "motherhood" as the proper role of women for the sake of society's stability turns the assumption on its head when women make motherhood subversive.

The same dynamic appears in the actions of three seemingly transgressive women of the Bible—Lot's unnamed daughter who becomes the mother of Moab and the ancestor of Ruth (Genesis 19:4–9, 30–38); Judah's daughter-in-law Tamar who becomes the mother of Perez and the ancestor of Boaz (Genesis 38), and Ruth. In each separate story of these women, the conventional urgency of wanting motherhood empowers deeply unconventional change. Even more unexpected, the three stories are linked by threads that are almost invisible—but not quite. The gossamer threads of connection strengthen each separate story into an epic of ironic transformation.

These three women all draw on the biblical legal rule ("levirate law") that if a husband dies without having fathered any children, his widow is entitled to marry and have children with his brother. If the brother refuses, he is subject to public contempt.

In the first of the three cases, after the explosive destruction of Sodom and Gomorrah, Lot's daughters (who have escaped along with Lot) are convinced that all the men in the world are dead, and in order to have children they get their father drunk and have sex with him. The child that is born to one of them is named Moab (which could be understood to mean "from daddy"). He becomes the head of a tribe and the ancestor of Ruth the Moabite.

We will come back to Ruth. Meanwhile, long after the generation of Lot's daughters, one of Joseph's brothers, Judah, marries one of his sons to a foreign woman, Tamar. Judah's son dies, with no children. In accordance with the law, Judah marries Tamar to his second son. But he too dies, leaving no children. Under the law, she is entitled to marry a third brother. But Judah fears she is jinxing his offspring and prevents a third marriage.

Tamar knows that she is entitled to have children by some member of this family. She pretends to be a prostitute, seduces Judah himself to sleep with her, and has twin children by him. Judah is on the verge of burning her at the stake for adultery, when she explains what she has done. She invokes an ancient version of the #MeToo challenge by a subordinate woman against a powerful man who has already abused her—first by breaking the law to deny her the social legitimation of bearing a child, and then by threatening to abuse her far more badly by burning her to death.

The #MeToo challenge works: Judah exclaims, "You are more righteous than I," cancels the execution, and treats her and her children as respected members of the community. So she, like Lot's daughter, by invoking a peculiar version of the levirate law, has turned the "subjugation" of women into an instrument of empowerment.

One of Tamar's children becomes the ancestor of a prosperous Israelite landholder, Boaz. Yes, the same Boaz who connects with Ruth the Moabite. Ruth's Israelite husband has died, leaving her childless. She, with Boaz's cooperation, appeals to a far-fetched version of the same law about a childless widow, finds that Boaz is a distant kinsman of her dead husband, and uses the law to marry him and have a child.

So these three women, all outsiders to the Jewish people, have stretched the law beyond its normal understanding in order to bring their children into the world. Then the story of Ruth goes out of its way to announce that Ruth's own children will become the ancestors of King David—and they do. Since Jewish tradition insists that the descendants of David will give rise to the Messiah (and Christian tradition specifically mentions Ruth as an ancestor of Jesus), in both traditions these three transgressive women are said to make possible the peaceful transformation of the world.

In this complex, interwoven tale, there is a subterranean assertion of what the Psalmist says in open song: "The stone that the builder rejected will become the cornerstone of the Holy Temple." The women who are "supposed" to be subordinate have subversively turned history around.

Notice that each separate story breaks the rules, and their culmination becomes a vision of Messianic time—which also "breaks the rules," for ultimate good. As if to say, a drizzle here, a drizzle there—and suddenly the raindrops will turn into a river.

How did the biblical text evolve into this effort to go beyond itself? The thread that tied the separate stories together was the Book of Ruth. And many modern scholars understand Ruth as a polemic in a major political/spiritual debate: a debate about the boundaries of the Jewish people and a debate about the role of women in those boundaries.

When the Jews who had been taken into Babylonian Captivity were permitted by the new Persian Empire to return to the Land of Israel and were handed power over those Jews who had never left, the returnees faced a question. Many of the men they met "back home" had married women who were not Jewish. Could this stand? Could the culture stand it?

The leaders decreed that all "foreign" women must be divorced. The Book of Ruth seems to have been an attack on this draconian policy. Its heroine was an outsider, and she became the forebear of King David. Should "foreign" women really be forbidden?

In other words, an actual struggle in the body politic led to an amendment in the sacred text. And then the sacred text remained a thorn, at least a puzzle, in the body politic. We see an interplay between sacred text that grows itself beyond itself and communal change that reshapes old forms into new paradigms.

This is the same process I have mentioned in explaining my own searching in the biblical tradition for pointers beyond the biblical tradition. Augustine said the sin of Eden made all human sex into a sin, and women became the incarnation of that sin and must therefore be kept subordinate. But many religious thinkers today say that is not so, and some of us say that the real sin of Eden was subjugation of the Earth. This process grows in a spiral: Social change enters and reframes the sacred text, and as our understanding of the text changes, the reframed text helps us take another step in reshaping a society where women freely lead.

How did this process, this spiral, start? For some, the rejection of "Women must be subordinate" began inside the text, in passages like the midwives, Miriam, Pharaoh's daughter. But for many it began with those who rejected the "sacred" text precisely because the text seemed unjust, unsacred. (The text was still powerful, demanding resistance to itself.)

As this secular feminist movement grew, women and men who still resonated with the text heard the *shofar* of justice ringing out in secular music. They grew clearer about where and how the text was/is unjust and began to search the text for clues and hints of transformation.

I remember the moment when my daughter, at a family Seder that was using the text of my "radical" Freedom Seder, found herself at a passage my father had asked her to recite. The passage referred to God as "He." My daughter read it as "She." Most of the boys at the Seder table erupted. My father, her grandfather, waited for the raucousness to calm. Then he firmly said, "I asked Shoshana to read the passage. She gets to read it as she likes." I was left, startled, to realize that my own justice-committed Freedom Seder still had left in it some passages that to her seemed clearly unjust. So I needed to wrestle with Torah yet again. "Politics" changes the Spirit; the Spirit changes politics.

So I found myself dancing again with the sacred, with pronouns for God and with practices for men and women. Where women freely lead through love, men must freely "wife" and "mother" lovingly. They must join in rearing children, housekeeping households. Where women—like our pioneer Ruth on the threshing floor—feel free to lovingly initiate a sexual relationship and explore whether that will be acceptable, consensual men must learn to lovingly explore, not dominate.

If we wistfully look through biblical texts to see a world like this, we find it. It is envisioned in the heart-opening poetry of the Song of Songs. So let us look further into how this process worked—or didn't—in the Bible's outlook on the sacred or the sinful roles of women.

The Song itself was clearly well known in Jewish life but hardly sacred. It was evidently being sung in "wine-houses"—what we might call "nightclubs"—as torch songs evoking musky sexuality. (How do we know this? I'll explain how in a moment.) Yet there were some people who thought it was a holy text. The question bubbled without a resolution.

The argument came to a head on a revolutionary day in the history of the Sanhedrin, the combined legislative /judicial/religious decision-making body for Jews who lived under Roman rule. The day was so astounding that later the Talmud says, "Whenever we say 'that day,' that is the day we mean!"

The Sanhedrin's chairman had poured contempt on one of its members who had disagreed with him. The chairman literally ordered the dissident to stand in a corner like a disobedient child. But the assembled rabbis began to chant, "Resign! Resign!" And the chairman did.

In that atmosphere they then proceeded to take up some burning questions that had long been stymied in a stalemate. Four hundred students who had been rejected from membership in the sacred academy of rabbis were welcomed. And interestingly, another burning question was also about boundaries —and the tribe of Moab. Could any of their males be welcomed into the Jewish people? The answer was Yes.

And then they took up the question, is the Song of Songs a sacred text? Some of the rabbis thought the notion was ridiculous. God's Name is nowhere mentioned in the entire text. And it is filled with nakedness—the same nakedness that Adam and Eve and everyone since correctly realized was shameful. It was a provocation to illicit sex, with barely a reference to marriage, and not a word on procreation. How could it stand alongside the Psalms, the painful story of Job, the pleasant tale of Ruth, and her marriage to Boaz?

But in the rebellious atmosphere of "that day," Akiba spoke. He said three things:

- that all the Writings were holy, but the Song of Songs was the Holy of Holies;
- that it was holiest precisely because God's Name was not mentioned in it; and

- that the day on which the Song was created was of equal worth to the day on which all the rest of the world was created.

In Akiba's generation, Rome had already destroyed the Temple and of course its innermost chamber. For the rabbis, sacred words of Torah, prayer, and midrash had replaced the body-centered Temple. Akiba was asserting that the Song was at the very heart of the sacred words. That gave new heart to the rabbis, and maybe to the people as a whole.

Akiba carried the day, "that day." The Sanhedrin voted that the Song was sacred. And on the same day, they voted to prohibit its being sung in the bawdy "wine-houses" of the day. If sacred it was, then erotic it was not.

What is more, the Song beyond all Songs became the heart of the religious experience for many mystics in Jewish, Christian, and Muslim traditions. Many of these mystics treated the Song as a joyful celebration of love not between a man and a woman but between—for Jews, God and Israel; for Christians, Christ and the Church; for Muslims, God and the individual ecstatic Muslim poet.

But the Song itself shows us the free and loving interplay of men and women; shows us a poetry led and probably written by a woman; shows us a spirituality not managed by the clock and calendar, as is the spirituality of the (male) rabbis, but rather governed by the principle, three times repeated, "Do not rouse love or lovers till they please."

This is all because the Song celebrates the joyful freedom and responsibility of women. The Song does not celebrate a perfect world. In its music is the screeching note that the men of the city beat and strip the loving woman. The Song celebrates a world imperfect but almost a black-and-white photographic "negative," a reversal of the reality we know. In our world, subjugation and violence and injustice appear almost everywhere; compassion and love arise in moments, bubbles. In the Song of Songs, the balance is reversed. It is almost as if the Song is saying, this is not "Utopia, Nowhere Land." We can make it real, if we try.

And it is no accident that at last we can see the Bible in this transformed way. For if we are looking for a Just-So story of our own, the question now must be "Women are moving from a place 'outside' to the inner spaces of the human race. Why?"

And just on cue arises this transformed "Just-So" understanding of the Bible and its holiest space, the Song.

What are we to make of this? Do we dare turn on its head the obvious biblical teaching of male supremacy?

I think we must. The Bible calls on us to read it, calling on us to go beyond what seems to be itself. The self-transforming naked-nakeder-nakedest Snake was right, and wrong: right to say we will not die if we transform ourselves; wrong to suggest that our self-transformation should take the form of gobbling up Earth's abundance; wrong to see our transformation in an act of subjugation, rather than an act of broader empathy.

What will happen if women are no longer subordinate? I think we are beginning to see some glimmerings of a future that was utterly unexpected. We can see stages of change as women became more equal in religious life and in society at large (I am presenting these as if they were chronological stages, but in actual life they often jumped around):

- First, women demanded, and began achieving, that they be treated as if they were men in roles that men had monopolized. Women could be political prime ministers and act like male political prime ministers. Women could be religious ministers and rabbis and act like male religious ministers and rabbis. (Not yet paid as much, and not yet as Catholic priests.)

- Second, women could take on those roles and bring quite different ways of acting in them. They might bring previous socializations to act unlike men—more nurturing, for instance. But all that didn't nullify the fact that more and more women were acting as if there were no difference between what women and men could do.
- Third, women could have sex with women and marry women as if their partners were men. That was a harder lift, since much of the definition of gender rested on sexual relationships; but at least in the eyes of the logical law, the case was reasonably clear. This was not as easy for families that had been raised around whole behaviors toward family members according to roles that were shattered. So it was often hard for families and friends to sever all connections with a person who "came out" as gay. But increasingly, as more and more women and men came out, family love and friendships won out despite established roles.
- Fourth, if all this were true and women could actually do anything men could—could actually lead in politics, fight in wars, marry women—what was the point of the categories anyway? Why ascribe to anyone that they belonged to one or the other?

It was reasonably expected—though surely not certain—that ending the subordination of women would soon after bring gay men and lesbian women into the Covenant. That did happen, and is still happening more and more fully. But who imagined that this shattering of the old assumptions about keeping women "in their place" might shatter the whole system of "places"? Might shatter the assumptions of binary gender?

Two men are all right. Two women are all right. Bisexual people are all right. But that "bi" reveals the hidden assumption that there are just two genders, just two flavors of active participants in sexual and social life. But people who cannot be pinned down to whether they are "men" or "women"? Suddenly Ursula LeGuin becomes Torah.

And almost fifty years after my daughter retaught me the freedom of the Freedom Seder, her child—my oldest grandchild—came to teach me once again that in our earth-round earthquake, the dance floor is still dancing. The grandchild who had been "she" became "they," moving beyond the gender binary.

And when I asked what might help me connect this, too, with Torah, they told me to read Judith Butler and Joy Ladin, and they were shocked that I knew nothing of them. So read I did: pushed not *by* books and theory but *into* books and theory; pushed into text by the "politics," by human interaction, by the quest for love renewed in a new context; shaken and entranced by Ladin's reframing of the Torah's first-born-brother stories—beyond my own theory of those stories, born from my struggles with my younger brother; shaken and entranced by Ladin's pointing to the Queer God who is beyond all "gender" categories—indeed, all categories.

Even before I read, I had begun to think that it was precisely the struggle to end the subjugation of women that had been the bridge into this even newer world.

I am not saying that individual women and men decided to see themselves as nonbinary in gender only because women were becoming freer. Nonbinary people had existed and lived their lives for ages past, mostly with little visibility and little public acceptance. Rather I am saying that the transformation of the roles of women in society at large freed people who had already been uncomfortable with binary definitions of their own gender to let their truer inner feelings flow more freely, more visibly, into the outer world.

This process—cascades of liberation—is not simple. There is a dynamic of privilege, even among the oppressed. The first people the women's movement began to liberate were heterosexual White women. It took a while for this process to begin liberating lesbians and Black women. The Stonewall uprising that multiplied and expanded the movement for gay liberation began, as my grandchild reminded me, when a Black trans woman threw the first brick at an oppressive cop. But the first numerous group of beneficiaries of that brick were White gay men, "most privileged" among those oppressed by sexuality and gender. It took years for that thrown brick to create the cascading ripples that even began to achieve liberation for Black trans women.

And today we see how powerful the backlashes to these waves of liberation are. In 2014, Gloria Steinem, speaking at The Shalom Center's celebration of "This Is What 80 Looks Like," said that moment in American society was like the moment when an abused woman walks out of the house. That is the moment most dangerous and most promising. The moment might bring violence, even murder, on her head from the abusive master. Or it might bring haven and community as she begins to birth a new life. The outcome depended on whether there was a movement, a community, ready to sustain her.

When Steinem said this, she thought it was a metaphor for all the movements just beginning to bubble in our lives. Who imagined a backlash leader who himself would boast about abusing women? Or that the women's movement would respond with yet another waterfall, #MeToo?

As the cascades of liberation followed, suddenly the Flood of Freedom became a myriad-colored Rainbow. Became—is still becoming—Torah in all its shades, not even merely seven as in most gay-rights Rainbow flags.

Oh, wait, the Rainbow has long been a Torah teaching! Years ago, thinking about the Rainbow as the symbol of recovery from the biblical Flood, I asked myself why Noah's Ark landed on Mount Ararat and the Rainbow appeared there. My answer was because Mount Ararat itself could see the great arc of many cultures in the "Fertile Crescent," in what for Torah was the world, that is, what we call the Middle East.

The Rainbow that appeared there was a gorgeous refraction, reflection, of that arc, a mirror of Life in all its variety, rekindled after a planetary holocaust. In the Rainbow House are many mansions.

That understanding of the Rainbow reenters Torah. Indeed, as we will see throughout this book, for thousands of years changes in the ethics and politics of society as a whole have affected debates about the meaning and future of Torah. That process is alive today. Sometimes the changes are small and incremental, as slight tremors move the holy ground beneath our feet.

When the tremors become a mighty quake, the changes may have to be profound and transformational, if they are to guide us toward pursuing justice, seeking peace, renewing Earth, and walking humbly in the winds of change, the Interbreathing Spirit.

At the end of this book, this journey, I point to the Song of Songs as "Eden for Grown-Ups," the Torah's effort to point toward its own transformation. In the Song beyond all Songs, the rigid boundaries of Talmud time are washed away. When is evening, when is morning? In the rush of love, the clock is washed clean of the numbers on its face. "Do not rouse love until the lovers please." Even in its seemingly binary heterosexuality, the Song is "queer." It is queer, for sure, to the biblical and rabbinic minds that choked on the words and melodies of the Song. That is why the fight over whether to accept the Song as sacred was so intense. That was from the perspective of the ancients. From our own Lookout Point today—even if women and men are becoming equal—is the Song still queer? I suspect it is.

So perhaps we can learn from the flowering of "beyond binary" in gender to think "beyond binary" not only about gender but beyond gender.

What might we learn? I do not know. I don't even have outrageous guesses. But I think we will all need to open our eyes wide to many rainbows of infinite colors.

What we thought were sins now seem life-giving possibilities. What were commands of hierarchy or even equality in rigid categories now increasingly seem sinful. The Scriptures reach beyond themselves, when we open our ears to hear. The only question is whether we can open our hearts to live.

3

The Real Sin of Sodom and the Sin of Lot —Today

The sin of Sodom was not what has become known in English as "sodomy." Yet the word—which bears a heavy electric charge of contempt and hatred—continues to stir up hatred and contempt toward men who find their best, or only, sexual satisfaction in sex with other men.

Most democratic societies have in our generation abandoned the idea that sex between two men is a crime. But interpretation of the Bible continues to matter, and the misconception that the sin of Sodom was sodomy continues to warp and pervert our culture away from empathy and love.

It is time for the very word "sodomy" to be dropped from our culture, and it is time for us to pay attention to what was the real crime of Sodom. What gave rise to the mistaken and hatred-laden notion that Sodom's sin was rampant homosexuality, and that for this sin it was destroyed by a Flood of Fire (Genesis 18–19)?

When Abraham's nephew Lot offered hospitality to two travelers, the people of Sodom were enraged. They besieged Lot's home, demanded that the two foreigners be given them to rape, to humiliate them, and warned Lot against hospitality.

This is a lot closer to the torture of prisoners at Abu Ghraib or the abuse and deportation of foreigners without trial than it is to the behavior of gay lovers.

The two foreigners turned out to be "angels," meaning they were messengers from God. The message they carried was clearly a warning, a crystallization, of God's love of welcoming strangers and God's disgust at hatred of foreigners. It took an obsession with sex and fear of sex among some Christian thinkers to turn the Bible's meaning upside down.

The biblical story itself, and practically all Jewish commentary and interpretation, make clear that the sin of Sodom was not rampant homosexuality but rampant rage and violence toward foreigners, immigrants, and the poor.

That line of thought began with the Prophet Ezekiel, bridging the seventh and sixth centuries BCE. He said (16:49–50), "Now this was the sin of your sister Sodom: She and her daughters were arrogant, overfed and unconcerned; they did not help the poor and needy." This understanding has continued for 2,500 years, into rabbinic thought till our own day.

Indeed, there is an often-repeated on-point story about an eighteenth-century rabbi, the Vilna Gaon, a genius of rabbinic knowledge and wisdom who taught in Vilna, Lithuania. One version of the story is told by our own contemporary, Rabbi Jeff Salkin.

> The Vilna Gaon had an honorary seat on the Council of Lithuania, also sometimes called the Council of Four Lands. One day, a member of the council proposed that it either end or greatly reduce the influx of Jews immigrating into Vilna. These immigrants were often terribly poor, and they were coming from the east because the Jewish community of Vilna had a relatively good social and economic safety net for the poor. That is what the councilmen wanted to destroy. At that moment, the Vilna Gaon rose to leave the meeting.

> "But, rabbi," said a council member, "we need your comment on this proposed new legislation."
>
> "You only need me if we are going to be discussing new legislation," the Gaon replied. "This isn't new. They tried it in Sodom years ago."

I am not suggesting that this misuse of the story of Sodom was the only reason for Christian hostility to male–male sex. There was, after all, an explicit biblical prohibition (Leviticus 18:22; 20:13) and traditional Judaism as well as Christianity mostly accepted that prohibition. (Not entirely—there were male–male erotic poems written by great Torah scholars in Al-Andalus from the tenth through the thirteenth centuries.) Only recently has that prohibition been abandoned by most Jews and many Christians, and even now, some Jewish and Christian communities rooted in the Hebrew Scriptures continue to enforce the prohibition.

Why the prohibition in the first place? I think there were two underlying reasons.

One was the Bible's acquiescence and affirmation of the subordination of women. What does the prohibition say? "A male shall not lie with a male as with a woman." If the biblical assumption is that a woman must be subordinate, then what would happen if a male were to treat another male as if he were a woman? Which partner in such a relationship would dominate, and which would be subordinate? For biblical society, the system would explode in self-contradiction. The small society of the family would break down and—the Bible imagines—the larger society would disintegrate as well. And that calculation explains as well why biblical tradition is simply uninterested in sexual relations between two women. Since the Bible sees both women as subordinate, it thinks that their relationship, far from blowing a gasket, does not even turn the computer on.

The second reason was the intense commitment to having children that pervades the Hebrew Bible—beginning with the command "Be fruitful, multiply, fill up the earth, and subdue it" (Genesis 1:28). (It is interesting that this sentence, with its grandiose vision of the human mission, echoes the painful vision at the end of Eden. This sentence closely connects birthing with ruling the Earth. The end of the Eden story closely connects painful childbearing with being ruled by the Earth.)

Beyond this overarching command, the Hebrew Bible is filled with stories of the failure of women to have children, their own sorrow and humiliation and the sorrow of their husbands at being childless, and the extraordinary measures some of them went to in order to reverse what seemed to be their fate.

There are the story of Abraham and Sarah's willingness to involve Hagar as a surrogate mother for the childless Sarah, similar stories of Rachel and Leah, and the story of childless Hannah's humiliation and her triumphant prayers for a son. There is the very existence of the levirate law to make sure a childless widow had a second chance at childbearing, and the amazing stories we have already recalled of how the levirate law worked toward the creation of the Davidic monarchy and thereby even toward the hope of Messianic deliverance.

There is even the stark fear of national childlessness, brought on by Pharaoh's effort to murder all male babies, and the salvation of the nation by the extraordinary resistance of midwives and the rescue of the baby Moses.

So on those grounds, male–male sex seemed, in the Hebrew Bible and even into the rabbinic tradition, a betrayal of the people's future.

In Christian thought from Augustine on, the importance of procreation was underlined by hostility to all forms of sexual pleasure. Male–male sex did not even have the saving grace of procreation; so sex purely for pleasure seemed anathema.

If these two reasons were the roots of forbidding male–male sex, then it is not surprising that the prohibition itself is weakening.

Now that social change is empowering women and the subterranean impulse of the Bible toward the equality of women is becoming real, the prohibition on subjugating "a man as with a woman" loses force.

And in our era, human overpopulation is endangering thousands of species that end up with no turf on which to flourish, even though they are crucial to the planetary ecosystem and greatly benefit the human species. So the focus on multiplying even more human beings loses force. As a result, male–male and female–female sexualities become as sacred or unsacred as male–female sex—sacred when consensual, when done with respect, and at best with love; unsacred when free choice, respect, and love are absent.

Once again, we see that while religious traditions affect and change the social systems that honor them, it is also true that changes in the social systems, which may arise for reasons beyond the explicit purview of religion, can change the ancient texts. And then the new interpretations of the ancient wisdom feed back into changes in society as a whole.

What is even more an earthquake in the old assumptions, these changes lead beyond themselves. What is male, what is female? Is that binary map sufficient to describe reality or enough to describe a joyful society? The very assumption that gender is binary is shaking as we explore more deeply these "new" realities. (This is new only in public visibility, not in physical and emotional reality.)

We face a new set of questions: Are people who shake off the old definitions "strange"? "Queer"? Do we treat them with the true sin of Sodom, hatred of strangers, or do we pursue new understandings of the biblical command to love the stranger?

Indeed, the most profound and cogent religious response to "Be fruitful, multiply, fill up the earth, and subdue it" may well be, "Done! Now what?" In other words, the entire epoch in which the human race strove to expand its power over the planet may now be over, and the need for another aspect of Torah may have become central. Discovering what that new religious vision is, and beginning to embody it, is what it means to dance in God's earthquake.

So much for the sin of Sodom! But there is another strand in the story to which neither Jews nor Christians have paid much attention until recently. It might be called the sin of Lot. He was Abraham's nephew, an immigrant to Sodom who, like his uncle, held as a high value the welcoming of foreigners as guests.

Faced with a mob of Sodomites enraged that Lot had made his home a nest of immigrants and refugees, Lot offered his own daughters to be raped by the mob, in order to calm their rage against his foreign guests. In a first and second and third reading of Lot's offer to let the mob rape his daughters, if they will leave his foreign guests unharmed, today we are horrified on two levels. First, that Lot is willing to subjugate women as if they were merely disposable means to a presumably worthy end. Living as we do in the midst of an uprising of women who have been abused and raped by powerful men—often men of talent whose brilliance has been treated as a reason to ignore their crimes—we may at last hear arising from the Bible the pained and angry "#MeToo" of Lot's daughters. Second, that in order to protect the foreigners Lot is willing to sacrifice and destroy his own family.

This is exactly Sodom turned upside down. The citizens of Sodom who surrounded Lot's house and threatened to rape or kill him and his guests are so obsessed with protecting their own city, their own jobs, their own culture that they are willing to wreak havoc upon foreigners. Lot, on the other hand, is so obsessed with protecting his guests that he is willing to wreak havoc on his own family.

Neither of these is a just or sacred solution to the tensions that often erupt between some "natives" and some "immigrants."

According to the story, once it becomes clear that not even ten just and decent people live in this hate-filled town, the Divine Breath of Life, the Wind of Change, becomes a Burning Hyperhurricane—so incensed at Sodom's hatred of outsiders that the city is destroyed.

Lot survives, but his lot is not so pleasant. His wife dies as collateral damage in the disaster. As we have already seen, the daughters, whom he had offered up as mere objects, think that all the other men in the world have died in the Flood of Fire. So they turn Lot into an object—just as he had done with them—by getting him drunk to make him father their children. Another kind of rape!

Today, many countries around the world have governments or strong political parties that commit the "sodomite" sin of hating and subjugating foreigners, the poor, outsiders in order to benefit the people Ezekiel named as "arrogant, overfed and unconcerned."

And in many countries around the world, Lot's daughters are still in danger. With or even without governmental approval, many women are met with violence to mollify those who fear the loss of old certainties: "honor killings" of women who choose their own lovers or husbands or even are raped, women trafficked for sheer profit or by their own desperate families on the verge of starvation, women forced into sex by outright violence or by fear of losing their jobs.

The story warns the citizens of all our countries that if we let ourselves be consumed, like Sodom, with fiery hatred of outsiders or like Lot, with brutal threats to our home born, we will bring fiery destruction on our own heads.

Is it magical thinking to imagine that hatred of foreigners could bring a Flood of Fire on our own country? Not magic, not at all. For efforts to inflame fear, contempt, and hatred of immigrants bespeak the same attitude that inflames fear, contempt, and hatred for some country defined as the enemy. We hear governments threaten to engulf these enemies in "fire and fury." Would this Fire stop there?

And if we take the story as a serious teaching, it is also warning us not to behave like Lot. Not to subject "our own" family, our own community, to humiliation and despair for the sake of "others." Just as the sin of Sodom brings disaster on the city, so the sin of Lot brings despair upon his family. If we behave like Lot, we are liable to suffer as he did. Just as his own daughters humiliated him, so we will face some of "our own" who will turn in bitterness against us.

We today are living in the ugly midst of the underlying argument: Protect one's own city, own family, at the cost of shattering the lives of immigrants and outsiders? Or protect the outsiders at the cost of shattering one's own city, one's own family? The famous tension between "particularism" and "universalism."

It seems to me that there are two major syndromes that can lead whole societies into this mistake. One is the pattern of turning the bitterness of one's own oppression into readiness to oppress someone else. The second is meeting not oppression but what seems an existential challenge on a field of equals. Let us look at each of them.

The first is lifted up by the Bible even as it struggles against the pattern. Some thirty-six times, the Torah implores us: "Love your neighbor as yourself!" "You shall not wrong a stranger or oppress him, *for you were strangers in the land of Egypt.*" We must act justly, compassionately, even lovingly toward the "foreigner" among us because we know what it was like to be foreigners, slaves, and pariahs under Pharaoh in the Land of Narrowness.

Many who seek to persuade us of the surpassing importance of this teaching point to the repetition of the command so many times. But the multiple repetition also points to something else that is not so obvious, and rarely becomes a focus for our thinking: Why did the command have to be repeated so often? Surely not because the people were obeying it. If I must again and again and again repeat the same teaching to my children, it is precisely because they are ignoring me.

For after all, what is the likeliest response of a people that has been newly freed from utter subjugation—torture, murder, genocide? Almost certainly, the impulse to take sufficient power to make sure it can never be made to suffer these torments again. Most likely, the oppressive experience of slavery under Pharaoh was a reason to press down anyone who might conceivably endanger these runaway slaves. A reason to raise their fists, saying, "Never again—not us!"

We know that this is indeed one response of those who are suffering from posttraumatic stress or from having been abused. Many then reenact the abuse on others, in order to make sure that having been victimized and traumatized once, they will not ever again be so treated.

One of the clearest examples of this reaction is the response of many Israeli Jews to the history of trauma in the Holocaust. Even those who were not themselves survivors have been shaped by the culture around them, even by the altered genes within them, by the continuing fears they feel. And that is the response that is poisoning the heritage of the Holocaust in the culture that has powerfully shaped and been shaped by the Jews who are citizens of Israel.

The inner response of abusing others to prevent the abuse of one's self is strengthened when the traumatized heir of being abused finds outsiders continuing to threaten danger or death. So for Israeli Jews, the nerve of fear was plucked again and again because they were confronted from the beginning by enemies who saw themselves as resisting an invasion of their lands and cultures by an outside force.

So for Israeli Jews and their Palestinian and other Arab neighbors, there followed generations in which Holocaust fears and *Nakba* fears (the word used by Palestinians to denote the "disaster" of the creation of Israel) reinforced each other. The injunction to respect and love the foreigner because of "having one's self known the heart of the foreigner" failed to win the heart of either people, as the experience of having been abused was heightened again and again. Even as the power of Israeli Jews grew, the fear of attack was fed by reality just enough to feed the sense of needing to increase their own power more and more. Increasingly, this became the power to subjugate, not only to defend.

Among American Jews, on the other hand, the shadow of the Holocaust had a profoundly different effect. Most American Jews after World War II felt surrounded not by enemies but by friendly neighbors. Most of their non-Jewish "neighbors" saw the Holocaust as a gigantic magnifying glass and mirror to their own anti-Semitism and their own racism, a warning of what such fear-filled hatred can lead to. So their impulse for seventy years after World War II was to safeguard Jews and to take the first baby steps toward embodying antiracist measures in law. That kind of energy also affected the international community and its adoption of measures to prohibit torture, to protect refugees, to define and criminalize genocide, and to adopt the Universal Declaration of Human Rights.

The tendency to safeguard Jews, we are in the midst of discovering, has begun to be frayed at the edges by more recent events. In response to globalization, multiculturalism, and a sense of economic and cultural marginalization of communities that saw themselves as "the real America," "the real Britain," and so on, many of the older strands of citizenry begin to feel Forgotten. And then, especially if politicians arise who fuel that energy, it can erupt into rage against the Other, the "New." Put Them down. Throw Them out. Including the Jews, and for some White nationalists, especially the Jews. Because it is the Jews, so the thinking goes, who nourish new power for otherwise weak and feckless people.

Meanwhile, some Jews become fearful in this renewed sense of vulnerability from attacks by major power centers and by those these White nationalists incite. One response is to unite in solidarity with others threatened by white nationalism. That response could carry the danger of enacting the sin of Lot. That is, preparing to allow the victimization of one's own community in order to forestall the victimization of others who are even more vulnerable. So far, I see few occasions when Jews have allowed that to happen.

Another response is to focus in fear against not the greater power of White nationalists but against expressions of anti-Semitism by people with far less power than the White nationalists.

And—another "meanwhile"—some Jews in power, whether motivated by fear, by generational trauma, or by the thirst for even more power, cheerfully join in subjugating real or imagined enemies. They join in the sin of Sodom—hatred of and aggression against the Other.

The Torah reminds us again and again that even if we keep coming back again and again to this way of acting, it was and is a mistake. Morally, ethically, and practically, it is a mistake. But knowing it is mistaken does not make it go away. Repeating the lesson dozens of times does not make the behavior stop.

What then? More attention to the teaching itself: "Love your neighbor as yourself." *As yourself.* Neither Sodom nor Lot. How do we affirm the community that has always thought it was the heart of our society, and in the same breath affirm the community that makes a new appearance, has a new presence, even if it has for centuries been present—but socially invisible? Ignorable? Of no account? In America, Native communities, Blacks, Latinos, Muslims, even women. In France,

Muslim women wearing hijabs. In Britain, Indians, Pakistanis, Jamaicans, Poles.

Sometimes when I speak with a church, a mosque, a synagogue, I try an experiment about invisibility. "How many of us this evening recognize the name of John Lewis?" Almost everybody knows who this icon of the civil rights movement is, how he was beaten almost to death for struggling to end racial segregation in the American South, and has lived his way into a special role in the US Congress. A role of deep respect.

Then I ask, "How many of us this evening recognize the name of John *L.* Lewis?" Very few people raise their hands. In the 1930s and 1940s, John L. Lewis was a front-page hero to workers, anathema to bosses and owners. He was the fierce leader of the United Mine Workers and the key founder of the CIO—the militant federation of industrial unions. He came out of the working class himself, and for the sake of workers in West Virginia challenged even the president of the United States, by leading strikes that interrupted the flow of a crucial strategic commodity, coal, in the midst of a global war.

John Lewis is Black. John L. Lewis was White. Both of them were insurgents against corporate control of America. One of them focused on challenging the racism that for centuries had subjugated Blacks and made it easier for corporate interests to divide workers from each other. The other focused on economic exploitation of both White and Black workers.

What would it mean to honor them both? To affirm them both as cultural heroes and to affirm the political stances of them both? Could the "new" constituency of Blacks and the "old" constituency of the White working class both affirm, "Love your neighbor—that is, each other—as yourself"?

Is it possible to have both compassion for the traumatized sufferers who out of trauma impose suffering on others, and insistence, as the Torah says, that this response is NOT wise, NOT permitted?

What might be a stance in feeling, thought, and action that might lead to a decent outcome? Does the Torah give us any hint of that kind of approach?

It does, in the bargaining between God and Abraham over whether Sodom should be destroyed in the first place.

Abraham's challenge to God hints at a resolution: If even a small minority of Sodom held fast to fairness and to empathy, there would be no destruction. But without ten such people, just barely large enough to be a community of action, there would be no way to redeem the city from its own destructiveness.

And this is exactly what the Torah says God has in mind. For God begins the process by letting Abraham in on the secret plan to punish the crimes of Sodom—wiping out the city.

Why has God singled out Abraham? According to the Torah, precisely because God sees Abraham as both the progenitor of a sacred people and the bearer of blessings to all peoples.

And Abraham responds!—by validating God's calling on him to become a blessing to all the families, peoples, cultures of the world.

Abraham tries to protect and defend even this nasty foreign city. "What about the decent, innocent folk who live in Sodom? Should the innocent be punished with the guilty? Is that what justice means? *Shall not the Judge of all the world do justice?*"

The Abraham who is to be the progenitor of a "particular" community—Yisrael, the "Godwrestling" folk, the Jewish people—is the same Abraham who tries to protect a foreign city from God's wrath.

This resolution does not call for a "balance" between the "particularism" of defending one's own and the "universalism" of defending the others. Rather, it calls for a synthesis. The "particularist" hero becomes the "universalist" prophet. The "universalist" prophet becomes the "particularist" hero.

Each role, taken on in full commitment, empowers and enriches the other role. Or rather, they are one role, not two, not "other." How do we resolve this collision in the spirit of the Torah's tale? I have two suggestions.

First, what sounds simple but is really hard: open our ears to the pain at the heart of both positions. And imagine not only "listening" but acting. Imagine the nuts and bolts of an economic and cultural resolution that looks beyond collision into transformation. Jumps beyond the box.

For example, what if we remembered that immigration does not begin at the Rio Grande? It begins much earlier, much further south, in poverty, frustration, fear.

What if we went to the roots of that despair? At one level, that would mean recognizing the responsibility of the US government and major US corporations for the social disruption in parts of Mexico, the Caribbean, and Central America that has turned into uncontrollable violence and spurred waves of migration. Perhaps even more important, beyond blame, would be a US decision to heal the disruption no matter who or what caused it.

What if our rich United States were to invest in grassroots prosperity creation in Mexico and Central America? Through "maximum feasible decision-making" by Ezekiel's "poor and needy," could we make sure that they themselves are making their own societies lifegiving and abundant?

That kind of investment might make it unnecessary for desperate people to flee to the US from their own homes, neighbors, and cultures for the sake of calm neighborhoods, decent schools, honorable and well-rewarded work. That might well mean paying for these investments by increasing taxes on Ezekiel's "arrogant, overfed and unconcerned" in the US. It might mean no longer importing peons so frightened and so ill-treated that they are desperate to work on profit-hungry US corporate farms at disgusting wages and working conditions. To honor and affirm Latin American lives would no longer mean demeaning the lives of working-class US Americans. And vice versa.

Now let me take up the second kind of case where two groups of people meet and each feels challenged by the other, not traumatized by cruelty—and yet they end up enemies. As I go out to speak in many varied venues, I often get asked, "Why does religion so often lead to violence and hatred, even when it claims to teach love and compassion?"

This is how I answer. Imagine a simplified history of religions. Each one is born when a wise teacher, or a community of wise teachers, intuits the ONE, the Unity of All. Around this sage there cluster people who are joyful to have their hunger for a fuller sense of Wholeness to be fed.

And that means telling stories of Meetings with the One. It means creating rituals, ceremonies, regulations, festivals, music, chants, pictures, architectures, sculptures—all pointing toward the One. Generation after generation, this treasury of joy grows richer.

And then this community meets another group of people. They also claim to be reaching toward the One. But they have an entirely different, or even overlapping, set of stories, rituals, ceremonies, regulations, festivals, music, chants, pictures, architectures, sculptures.

There are two possible responses to this surprising discovery.

One is in shock and anger to shout out: "You are wrong! And what is even worse, you are lying! We know how to get in touch with the One, we have struggled for many generations to shape and use those channels, and they work! So your practices must lead you somewhere else, even to demonic powers. We must stop you, or our children will be lost and wandering adrift in dangerous waters!"

And the other? "How wonder filled, our world! The One is Infinite! And so there are many, many paths of life to celebrate that Unity. Teach us your ways, and we will teach ours. May we always feel the special joy that comes with family, what is 'familiar.' And may we also together learn to celebrate the Radiance that glows in many colors. If we listen, we can learn to embody in one body our inward hearts and outward eyes."

How do we learn to walk the path that is not fearful and violent, but open, curious, empathic? What practices can guide us there?

4

Hiding in the Holy: Love, Awe, or Idolatry?

You are not to make yourself a carved-out image of any figure that is in the heavens above, that is on the Earth beneath, that is in the waters beneath the Earth. You are not to bow down to them, you are not to serve them. For I, YHWH [Yahhh/Breath of Life] your God, am a zealous God.

—Exodus 20:4

Idolatry is an act the Torah views as the crucial sin—a direct challenge to the true God. The prohibition of acting in this way is encoded early in the Ten Utterances that the Voice speaks at Sinai (as above). Perhaps when this passage was written it meant to the ancient Israelites the physical act of bowing down to a physical object carved of wood or stone or metal. Today we might understand it more broadly: *Do not carve out a piece of the Great Sacred Flow and bow down to that carved-out partial piece as if it were the Holy One, the Unity.*

In this view, the carved-out part, the piece, might be a state, a form of government, a religious tradition or community, a set of assumptions about how to find the truth, your property that you think properly belongs to you, a system of technology. Why do I feel drawn to this broader definition of an "idol"? Does this approach add anything to other kinds of criticism?

Let me start by mentioning a few examples of what seem to me idolatries.

When some Muslims decided that a US military presence was contaminating the sacred soil of Saudi Arabia, and cleansing that soil required killing three thousand people in the Twin Towers, that act was the product of turning the love due sacred soil and sacred memories into idolatry.

When some "old-line" White Americans elevated their sense of a valuable culture into an Absolute that justifies contempt and violence toward other cultures, lifting the swastika beside the Confederate battle flag and allowing a neo-Nazi to commit murder, that violence was rooted in turning love of that culture into idolatry.

I am drawn by my own life experience to examine two other cases much more deeply. One of these is the way the Roman Catholic Church has dealt with cases of the sexual violation of children by priests and even by bishops during the last several decades. The other is the way many American and Israeli Jews have lifted up the government of the State of Israel, or the state itself, as an "Ultimate" that must not be criticized in any serious depth.

From my perspective, many holders of sacred office have turned the Church itself into an idol, and were willing to act atrociously against children and keep atrocious behavior secret because revealing it might damage the finances, political power, or public respect for the Church. Let me unfold more fully what I keep in mind as markers of idolatry.

How do we distinguish between something that is worthy to be valued and something that claims worship but is actually an idol that must not be worshipped? Note the Talmud story.

In the days when Rome ruled ancient Palestine, a Jew came to a rabbi, saying, "I have bought a home from a Roman. Behind the house is a pleasant pool of water, and at the water's edge there is a lovely statue of a woman. I think it may be the Venus whom some Romans worship. Is the statue an idol, so that I must destroy it?"

"It depends," said the rabbi. "If the statue was sculpted to add more beauty to the pool, it is a sculpture merely: Enjoy its beauty. But if the pool was dug to celebrate and glorify the statue, then it is an idol and you must destroy it."

So the quality of "idolness" does not inhere in any specific object, physical or institutional, but in the way people behave toward it.

This measuring stick may not be absolute. Garry Wills, who has written on prophetic religious compassion and destructive religious idolatry, has suggested that in American society, The Gun is what the Bible calls *Moloch*: a god who demands as offerings the mass murder of children and other human beings. But it is clear that Wills did not regard guns—the physical objects—in themselves as Moloch: he described as Moloch the whole apparatus of the Church of Gun, including the executive director of the National Rifle Association as its pope, mobilizing the ardent commitment of its worshippers.

On the other hand, in the 1980s, in response to the renewed nuclear arms race, Professor Ira Chernus of the University of Colorado suggested that an H-Bomb, simply by physically existing, is Moloch.

The Talmud tells another story that greatly enriches the process of discerning what is an idol. The story says that some of the rabbis went searching for one specific form of the *yetzer hara*, the impulse toward evil. The one they chose to hunt for was the impulse to idolatry, the impulse that breeds idolatry. They thought if they could find it, they could kill it—and thus end idolatry.

They hunted and hunted, and finally found it hiding in the innermost sacred place of the Holy Temple in Jerusalem: the Holy of Holies. In it, according to tradition, were the broken pieces of the original Ten Commandments, which Moses shattered when he beheld the Israelites cavorting around the Golden Calf. In it were the Tablets that followed when God forgave the people for their idolatrous sin. In it were some flakes of the miraculous Manna that showed a wandering, quarrelsome people that Earth could be abundant despite the mortal mistake Humanity had made according to the parable of Eden. Into this Holy of Holies could walk only one person, the High Priest, and then only at one moment every year: High Noon on Yom Kippur. And yet, and yet, in this utter serenity of holiness was also the impulse to idolatry.

The story warns us it may be easiest to turn something worthy and holy into an idol. I think it is exactly that process at work in regard to the Catholic Church and the government and/or State of Israel.

The Church has done and continues doing some extraordinary and sacred work. It has worked hard on behalf of the poor in America and on behalf of immigrants' rights. Many of its religious orders—especially those of women—have been deeply and creatively involved in work to meet the immediate needs of the poor, and sometimes in movements for deeper social change to achieve more justice, more peace. During the last several years its pope and some (but at this writing a minority) of its US bishops have galvanized support for preventing climate disaster. Moreover, for millions it provides spiritual and liturgical support at moments of profound life change and in everyday life as well.

Yet! Yet the very existence of that sacred work has been the reason that many in its hierarchy have given de facto indulgences from sin to its own clergy who sexually harassed and assaulted children (a historical irony, since it was formal indulgences granted for absolution from sin that sparked the Protestant rebellion).

Admiration for the Church as a sacred institution led many of its leaders to fear that public confrontation with sinful assailants would make scandal for the Church and weaken its moral authority. They lost sight of the reality that this deliberate blindness not only betrayed the moral mission of the Church but, when the world's blinders did finally fall away, led to exactly the scandal and loss of moral authority they feared.

The political clout of the institution, originally rooted in the assumption of its moral authority, then corrupted some public officials and journalists who refused to bring it to public account for fear of its power. So, parts of American society were infected with cynicism about precisely spiritual energy, honor, and honesty in general.

In these ways, love and respect for the Church became idolatry through the cover-up of sin. But what about the sin that began the process? How did so many of the clergy (a minority, but thousands in the clergy of many nations around the world) turn to using their power to bring trauma instead of love and inspiration upon children—and sometimes adults in vulnerable positions, like seminarians?

Some have suggested that the Church's Augustinian distaste for all sexual expression, only reluctantly approved in order to procreate children, was at the root of this tree of hostility to many forms of sex. And women could be singled out as the dangerous ones. Women were visibly the bearers of the fruit of sex. On top of that, the ancient misreading of the end of the Eden parable helped keep women in their subordinate place where society, generation after generation, had sent them. So keeping women out of the priesthood made sense.

If women and sex were a necessary evil, then the spiritual best of all imperfect humankind—that is, priests—should all be men and celibate. And insistence on an exclusively male, celibate clergy was quite likely to lead to a plague of sexual coercion, not just sexual abuse of children and of vulnerable adults, like nuns and seminarians, but of many whole categories of sexual expression. Horror at and punishment of all sexual expression that was not intended to birth children of course became horror at homosexuality, at birth control, at abortion, which canceled the only legitimate reason for having sex in the first place.

The parable of Eden claims to be speaking about the entire human race. So to whatever degree the Church reads the Eden parable as the story of sexual sin and Eve's subordination (sometimes more, sometimes less), it is caught within the belief that its own sexual ethic applies to all humanity. So, it feels called to legislate that ethic upon everyone else.

Is this version of its calling itself universal a way to make the Church an idol, because it assumes that only the Catholic Church has understood and proclaimed the only True Morality? Does it assign to one carved-out aspect of reality the moral values of the Infinite and diverse Flow of Life?

What happens when the Church, in a society where it has great power but not absolute power, tries to impose its ethic and its will on almost all American Catholic women who use birth control and affirm that its use accords with their own moral conscience? On non-Catholic women? What happens when it tries to impose its ethic and its will on the whole spectrum of GLBTQIA sexual and gender minorities? Upon women and men who claim or don't claim membership in the Church and who make their own choices about abortion?

Is there a connection between what we might call the Church's Higher Idolatry of claiming for itself a universally true sexual ethic, and its fall into the Lower Idolatry of covering up its violation of its own "pure and perfect" sexual ethic, asserting that the cover-up was sacred because its mission was so sacred, and no deep public criticism could be allowed to scratch or melt this perfectly beautiful statue?

For those inside the Church and for me and for many others in other spiritual, religious, or secular-ethical communities, this idolatrous dynamic poses serious questions of conscience and action.

- Should we cooperate with an institution when it works for good, despite its tolerance of systemic sin?
- Should those of us who are "outsiders" to the Church keep silent when the behavior of its idolaters bring—for many in our society—doubt, shame, and disgrace on the entire enterprise of religion and spirituality?
- Must we take what was happening in the Catholic Church as a signal to bring renewed and rigorous care and attention to the misuse of power within our own communities?
- Should we who have a different theology about sex, abortion, birth control, homosexuality, and the moral agency of women be specifically organizing inside and outside the Church to prevent its official theology from being turned into US law?

Aside from these questions that we who are "outside" the Church must ask ourselves, what changes inside the Church would be necessary to prevent its descent into making the Church itself an idol?

- Must the Church abandon the whole version of Eden as a story of sexual sin and the subordination of women?

- Must there be a vigorous moral and political reframing of the Church that values and guarantees internal freedom of criticism and debate?
- Must there be a profound organizational reframing to end the totally top-down decision-making of the Church?

To me it seems clear that not only Catholics but many of us from other spiritual, religious, and secular-ethical communities are affected, and must respond. Seek not to know for whom the bell tolls; it tolls for me—and thee.

So I have made clear how the dangers of idolatry in one American community not my own affect me, even though I am "outside" it. Now let me turn to the danger of idolatry in the American Jewish community, of which I am a conscious and active member.

For many American Jews, especially of my elderly generation, the State of Israel is indeed the "Holy of Holies," as the Talmud story names the place where the impulse for idolatry chose to hide.

That is because it embodied, at the beginning, both the value of physical protection for Jews after one of the most dreadful moral and physical assaults on a whole people in history, and the cultural and moral value of a place that seemed to offer renewal of a humane Jewish culture.

In America, almost all Jewish organizations were reshaped between 1948 and 1967 as affirmers, protectors, and defenders of the new State. For many American Jews at the grassroots and for many of their organizations, it became hard, even fifty or sixty years later, to assess the State in the light of changing realities.

So for many, it is emotionally and spiritually and intellectually hard even to raise the question whether the State is like the poolside statue in the Talmud story—made by human beings and subject to praise and criticism and even recasting by human beings—or an idol, to be worshipped at the risk of excommunication of anyone who fails to genuflect.

I think it is idolatry at work when the organized and undemocratically governed structure of most large organizations in the American Jewish "community" tries to make the State of Israel and even its government sacrosanct, and moves to expel critics of Israeli policy or of the State itself from Jewish life.

For me, there are three idolatrous deformities now being enforced on Israelis and increasingly on Jews elsewhere, and others as well, by the present government of Israel:

- The military occupation and oppression (including the blockade and repeated invasions of Gaza) of what could and should be the independent State of Palestine living peacefully alongside Israel;
- The legal and social elevation of the Jewish segment of the Israeli people to overlordship over other Israeli communities, and increasing repression of dissenters who condemn these two aspects of subjugation and repression; and
- The alliance of the present right-wing Israeli government, the present right-wing US government, some parts of American Jewish institutional structures, some European nationalist governments that are anti-Semitic at home and support Israel as a right-wing bulwark against Islam, and right-wing Christian fundamentalists who support a conquistador Israeli state. This alliance is increasingly seeking to ostracize, punish, and repress American critics of the Israeli government—Jews, Christians, Muslims, and assorted others.

All three endanger me and others who express a range of criticisms by posing threats from "outside" ourselves: as active citizens, by threatening us with the loss of a job or of donors and grants and of being welcomed as teachers even on unrelated questions; by threatening some critics with being refused entry to Israel and others even with prison in America if they take part in boycotts of Israel.

More deeply, these behaviors endanger me from "inside" myself; they pervert and try to control my sense of what being Jewish is all about. For I celebrate the sacred wisdom of the ever-growing, ever-unfolding Torah, and these behaviors poison the bloodstream of that Holiness. Those are the words that keep souring my tongue, my throat, my belly: *They poison the bloodstream of Torah.* They make the Breath of Life into a frozen carved-out idol.

There is much that is worthy and holy about the Israeli society that has been a refuge for some endangered Jews and has nurtured new forms of Jewish culture in many brilliant poets, filmmakers, and novelists.

I was delighted and enlightened when in 1982, a "secular" Israeli commission investigating the massacres of Palestinians at Sabra and Chatila insisted that even though Israeli soldiers were not themselves the bloody-handed killers, the acquiescence of their officers as they saw the massacres proceeding violated Torah—and required punishment.

By the same token, I was distraught when Baruch/Aror (Blessed/Cursed) Goldstein drew on the satirical Scroll of Esther to justify a Purim frenzy in which he murdered twenty-nine Palestinians prostrate in prayer in the mosque where lies the tomb of our common father Avraham/Ibrahim/Abraham.

What stirred me in both moments? I was deeply moved by the decision of even self-proclaimed secular Jews to see the compassionate wisdom in the Torah. And I was horrified by the ability of the Accursed Goldstein to make his machine gun into a midrash, poisoning the bloodstream of Torah by citing the festival of Purim itself (by implication, Esther 9:16) as the justification for pouring out the blood of innocents.

The Israeli government claims that it leads a Jewish State and embodies the will of the whole Jewish people. When the government lifts up the Torah of compassion, broadening the action of its Commission of 1982, it is bringing offerings of justice to the Holy of Holies.

When it gobbles up large chunks of Palestinian land for Israeli settlers; when its army and its settlers destroy Palestinian olive trees with impunity, in direct violation of Torah (Deuteronomy 20:19–29); when it blockades Gaza's people from jobs, travel, and fisheries for food; when it destroys Palestinian homes in East Jerusalem; when it imprisons foreign petitioners for asylum as refugees in direct opposition to the compassionate will of Torah (Deuteronomy 23:15–16)—and when it then demands obeisance from American Jews for all of this, should the authentic Jewish response be obedience—or sharp and deep criticism? Are the land, the State, the government still purely bearers of the Holy, or has the impulse to idolatry crept into power?

For American Jews to respond with silence or tortuous justifications is to turn love and admiration into idol worship.

Some may justify silence out of fear that criticism will weaken the holy sanctuary. But the deepest Jewish wisdom is that idolatry kills:

Psalm 115 warns, "The idols have noses but breathe not, eyes but see not, mouths but speak not, ears but hear not, hands but touch not, legs but journey not. Those who make them and those who put their trust in them become like them."

That is, their makers become dead like these dead idols that they make. The process of idol making deadens the idol makers: deadens their joy, their creativity, their connection with the Great Flow of Life; deadens their ability to dance in an earthquake.

What is the State of Israel? Is it something we have sculpted, intending that it embody compassion and creativity? Then when some claim it fails to do so, when some critics say the hands have become fists or even that the whole design is flawed, the sculptors must take the critique seriously. They must act to repair the flaws. They must even open themselves to hearing those who say the sculpture's design is so flawed that it must be replaced with a new instrument for compassion and creativity.

The critics may be right or wrong. But they must be heard, and then we make our judgment. Our judgment will be wiser if we listen. To wall the critics out, even to say that some of them, nitpicking, are legitimate but others, more questioning of the root, are not—that is, to put an impenetrable wall around our sculpture, to insist that all the pools of tears that have been shed for her are only forms of adoration. That makes the State into an idol. And idolatry kills. Godwrestling wounds, but idolatry kills.

What defines the difference between the true God and an idol?

- The willingness to challenge, to criticize: "Shall not the Judge of all the world do justice?" says Abraham to God, and won't let go until he hears a just decision (Genesis 18:25).
- The willingness to wrestle. "I will not let You go until You bless me," says Jacob the Heel, the Grabber, who at last has Wrestled with the God Who has created the impossible choice between stifling his own soul and robbing his brother. And he receives the blessing that he is and must be a "Godwrestler," *Yisrael*—and we name ourselves according to the blessed obligation. Choosing to be a people that Wrestles God, History, Reality (Genesis 32:23–33).
- The willingness to demand compassion, even though God's Own Self has proclaimed Divine Jealousy so

> intense it cancels out compassion. When God explained why He punished His people with a Death March into Babylonian Exile, our Mother Rachel rose up to confront Him, the midrash tells us (Eicha Rabbah 24).

What was God's explanation? "They were whoring after strange gods, and I am a Jealous God!"

"Jealous?!" said our Mother Rachel. "Jealous of dead sticks and empty stones? I was jealous of my real live sister. When my father, Laban, gave her as wife to my beloved Jacob, instead of me, I was so jealous that I prepared to shame her publicly for the deception. But my love and my compassion overwhelmed my jealousy, and I forebore. You claim to be the Jealous Holy One, and for this You would torture and destroy Your People? How dare you?!" And God, now more ashamed than jealous, relented.

No people dare to challenge an idol they have made, because no idol responds to being challenged.

Our ancestor Jacob wrestled God's very Self to get beyond his own destructive dilemma, his own seemingly obdurate reality. Through that ultimate Wrestle, he turned himself from a robbing, lying Heel to a compassionate Godwrestler.

For all of us who claim the name of "Israel, Yisrael, Godwrestler," as for our forebear Grabber Jacob, to become Godwrestlers means to ask, "Does the fulfillment of our own sacred identity require some who claim that name to rob our Palestinian cousins and lie to ourselves? Is there no way beyond that destructive dilemma?"

If we are serious about naming ourselves "Israel" after his transformed self, we must as the people Israel take on the task of wrestling with the seemingly obdurate reality of our own day, the task of moving beyond the destructive dilemma. But at least till very recently, most American Jews were unable to face Israeli Jews squarely and say that truth. And even now, most of the large organized structures of American Jewry are not only unwilling to say so, but are likely to expel from their midst American Jews who do say so.

Thus Hillel International, the organization intended to serve American Jewish college students, has imposed a set of political litmus tests on every local Hillel house on every campus. In doing so, it forces out of the Jewish community even—especially!—those Jews who question like Abraham, wrestle like Jacob, challenge like Rachel. Those Jews are possibly the lively future of the Jewish people, if the people need to learn to dance in God's earthquake.

And when some students responded by founding "Open Hillel," invoking the name and symbol of a great Jewish teacher known precisely for his openness to a wide range of ideas, "Hillel International" sued to prevent what it saw as a "trademark infringement."

This was not only an attempt at political oppression but an attempt at cultural kidnapping—annexing Hillel himself under State-of-Israel hegemony as if he were part of the West Bank (as if George Washington University were to sue every business, every college, every street-naming town or city, that named anything after President Washington).

By no means have all American Jews turned love or admiration for Israel the State, for the rebirth of Hebrew and the birth of a new creative film and literary culture in modern Hebrew, for the sanctuary for endangered or forgotten Jewish communities, into idolatry. And in the last decade, organizations have formed and begun to grow that try to keep alive the distinction between an unchallengeable idol and a beloved sculpture that must be repaired or redrawn or even melted down to create a new and more beautiful sculpture from that same holy metal.

Even those who think as Martin Buber and Henrietta Szold thought more than seventy years ago—that a "binational" State might be more "Jewish" in its ethics and its culture than a "Jewish" State that saw itself forced or seduced into oppressing others—need to be heard. They might be mistaken in our day as Buber and Szold now seem to have been in theirs—but perhaps our present crisis points to a grain of truth in those Prophets of seventy years ago.

We also face the troubling truth that not only some American Jews but some powerful branches of American Christianity have made the State of Israel into an idol.

At the theological level, for some, this is rooted in the apocalyptic imagery that only through a conquering Israel can the armies of God at Armageddon defeat the long-lived "satanic" forces of Islam, bring forward a warlike version of the messianic Christ, and—the irony!!—at last dissolve the stubborn Jewish refusal to affirm the messianic role of Jesus. What makes this vision ironic is that through "support" for the State of Israel, it hopes to end the Jewish people. What makes this vision idolatrous is that for the sake of this end goal, it shrugs away every murderous event along the way.

At the political level, there has emerged an alliance between some fundamentalist Christians, some supporters of a corporate-dominated America, some resurgent racists and White supremacists, and a small minority of Israelolatrous Jews. This alliance has offered the "Christian Zionists" a possible path toward political domination for their other priorities—especially the subjugation of women, sexual minorities, and sex itself.

Just as the Roman Catholic Church has tried to impose its sexual ethic on all Americans through national legislation and court decisions, the idolaters of Israel have urged the US government to use its power of grant making to colleges and universities to impose a ban on criticism of Israel, on the grounds that such criticism is a version of anti-Semitism.

What would it mean to turn the State and government of Israel back from idols that some of us worship into instruments that we have made and can reshape for the sake of justice, compassion, and peace? For the sake not only of the two peoples who live in this tiny sliver of a land but also of the Land itself, which modernist industrial nationalism has wounded in this slender slice of Earth as the One Round Earth has been similarly wounded?

Perhaps it means acknowledging that we can now see flaws in the very structure that were not apparent to most of us when the statue was first cast in bronze.

Perhaps we can draw on Torah itself to do this. The Torah that most Jews read on Rosh Hashanah is about the threats that our Father Abraham posed to the lives of both his children, Ishmael and Isaac. Those two iconic figures both communities acknowledge as the forebears of our peoples.

So perhaps on Yom Kippur we should complete the story, by reading the Torah (Genesis 25:7–11) of how the two estranged brothers came together in peace to bury their dangerous father. And perhaps Jews might meet on that Yom Kippur with Muslims, Arabs, Palestinians—to acknowledge the deadly mistakes that both our peoples have made and hear how we think we can do *tshuvah*—turning in peace to each other and to the God we both affirm.

And if this model has any redeeming value, perhaps it would be useful in conflicts in which the Jewish people are not a major partner. Just as one brand of bread proclaims, "You don't have to be Jewish to love rye bread," you don't have to be Jewish to love wry truth. Perhaps we could face the history of racism in America by creating a Day of Atonement, a Day of At-One-Ment, to repair that other sinful idol worship. A Day of Truth and Transformation that could, step by step, lead to Reconciliation. Perhaps the Fourth of April, the day on which Martin Luther King, Jr., was murdered.

Might going beyond the Jewish idolatry also take a more political form, rooted in a compassionate and mutually respectful religious outlook? Perhaps it means an alliance of American Jews, Muslims, and Christians to demand that the US government convene and chair an Emergency Conference on Peace in the Middle East, where the US lays out the regional peace settlement that includes a safe Israel and a safe Palestine.

Perhaps it means demanding that the Jewish Federations keep raising money for Israel and put it in escrow till there is a two-state peace treaty or a regional peace treaty.

Perhaps the people Israel might affirm a special relationship with a State of Israel that has a majority of Jews among its citizens—but/and might also insist that for the sake of Judaism and the Jewish future, such a state must not be a "Jewish State" but in actual fact, not just in rhetoric, a state of all its citizens. A state that is no longer an imperium ruling over another people.

As I write, more and more people are saying that the multiplication of Israeli settlers in the Palestinian West Bank and East Jerusalem has made the creation of two states politically impossible. If so, perhaps we can work out a cantonal decentralized state where various kinds of Jews and Palestinians can shape their cultures in their own ways, while exercising equal rights to decide the policies that only a single government can carry out.

Perhaps—

These suggestions are hints toward creativity and blessing. Hints toward wrestling. But only hints. I hope that no reader will get frozen onto either "pro" or "con" reactions to any of these specific ideas, hints. I list them only as examples of a great range of possibilities for creative examination. It is the process that will count. These hints are drawn from trying to examine the steps by which we can make the sacred into an idol and perhaps the steps to reverse the process. I think we can identify steps on the path toward idolatry, in both the cases I have been examining deeply.

In a community or an institution seen as sacred and crucial, some members begin to act in ways that deny its basic values. Perhaps they are expressing a repressed and forbidden need—as in some Catholic clergy required to be celibate. Perhaps they are expressing the need to assuage their fear of attack and their itch for triumph, as in some Israeli settlers on the West Bank.

At this stage, the violations may not yet be idolatry; they are ethical misdeeds. If they are seen, confronted, challenged, and ended, the sacred institution is doing its sacred job. If they are ignored, hidden, or celebrated for the sake of the safety and success of the institution, the institution is well on the way to making its sacredness into an idol. If criticism wells up but is prohibited, excommunicated, outlawed, then the living sacred body has been frozen into an idol, cut off from the Great Flow of the ONE.

How do we reverse this process? Beginning at the end, we must encourage open criticism and creative resistance toward all the specific misdeeds and toward the structure that protected them. Not "criticism" in words alone, but with our whole bodies, as in the metaphor of wrestling.

Already in the Jewish community there are waves of mostly younger people who vigorously oppose the Israeli occupation of Palestinian lands on the West Bank, East Jerusalem, and blockaded Gaza. Some of these folks cluster around supporting deep reforms of Israeli society and the conclusion of a two-state peace between Israel and a viable Palestine. Others have become convinced that the idea of a "Jewish State" inevitably leads to the practical result of a deeply flawed and domineering society. For these people, the logic of this conviction means calling for "BDS"—boycott, divest, sanction—pressures on Israel and the pursuit of a "one-state solution." For some sections of progressive politics, the danger has arisen that BDS might itself become an idol that cannot be debated or criticized.

The emergence of both these energies among Jews has made for some demands within and beyond the Jewish community for more crackdowns on critics of Israel. It has also emboldened some beyond the Jewish community to begin urging that the US government demand that Israel end the occupation.

In this case of the danger of idolatry I have explored as well as in the other, the one hiding inside the Roman Catholic "Holy of Holies," the results of the struggles are still uncertain. "Justice How?" or "Idolatry Now?"—the answers are "blowin' in the wind." Perhaps in the wind, the breath, the Holy Spirit that we all make by blowing breath of words and winds of change into the world.

Perhaps for us all, not only for the people who had the audacity to name themselves the Godwrestlers, the story of how a Jacob—a heel, a grabber, a thief, a liar—became a wrestler with God is the archetypal story we can all learn from.

Facing his own fear and guilt, questioning the very structure of the world in which for what he thought was God's sake he had become a heel, Jacob was able to receive a blessing, to become a blessing. Able to embrace his brother.

No longer to make his own identity an idol. No longer to make his fear his idol. No longer to generate from the sin of idolatry his many other sins.

Free to celebrate the God Who has eyes that See, Who has ears that Listen, Who has arms that Embrace, Who has legs that Walk an ever-changing path, who has a nose that Breathes. Who lives and gives life.

5

Renaming God: Toward an Ecological Worldview

You are not to take up the Name of YHWH your God for emptiness." (Sinai, one of the Ten Utterances.)

—Exodus 20:7

God spoke to Moses and said to him, "I am YHWH. I was seen by Abraham, by Isaac, and by Jacob as El Shaddai—Nurturing [Breasted] God. But by My Name YHWH I was not known to [grokked by] them."

—Exodus 6:2–3

Nishmat kol chai / tivarekh et-shimcha
Yahhhh eloheynu.
Hallelu-Yah, Hallelu-Yah,
Hallelu-Yah, Hallelu-Yah.

The Breath of all life praises Your Name
For Your Name Itself whispers all breath.
Hallelu-Yah, Hallelu-Yah,
Hallelu-Yah, Hallelu-Yah.

—The Shabbat Morning prayer book,
modified for and from a chant
by Joey Weisenberg

What is the Name Itself, anyway? And what is "emptiness"? Up front I want to say, I do not believe the Utterance at Sinai means that we should not say, "Oh my God!" or "Good God!" or "For God's sake!" I think it means something far more profound.

One way to look at this Teaching is to look back to when the Voice first names Godself, speaking to Moses in the Ever-Burning Bush. Moses's heart lights up in burning passion for the freedom of his people. His heart will not flame out, and yet is not burned out, is not consumed. (The whole story of Moses at the Bush is in Exodus 3–4.)

Another way to unlock this riddle is to look at a prayer of today and every day, the Kaddish prayer that arrives in rhythmic timing and also untimely to tremble at the edge of life and death. It begins by invoking God as "*shmei rabbah*," the Great Name.

"What is your Name, Most Holy One?"

"My Name is the Great Name," comes the answer.

"What? Who?"

There is a connection, a subterranean connection, between the sense of God that flies up like sparks from the Burning Bush, and the sense of God that is encoded in the Great Name. In order to uncover and trace the connection, let us begin by standing with Moses at the ever-burning Bush.

The Voice that arises like smoke from the fire tells Moses that he must return to the Egypt he has fled, to awaken the people and confront the Pharaoh. He must demand their freedom from slavery and their free passage back to their land of origin.

Moses stutters and stammers that he cannot speak well enough to represent either God or the people. And he warns that everyone will say, "Sez who? Who sent you?"

The Voice speaks out three Names as warrants for this moment of great daring.

First, "*Ehyeh Asher Ehyeh*." "I Will Be Who I Will Be. I Am Forever Becoming."

When King James appointed a committee to translate the Bible into English, they decided to translate this sentence as, "I Am That I Am." Since they were reporting to a king, it made sense to please him by suggesting that the universe was static. What king would like the universe to change and keep on changing?

But at the Bush, the Voice was addressing not a king but a revolutionary—someone who was being called to shake the very foundations of kingship. So the Hebrew—which was actually in the future tense—would say that the roots of the universe are Change. Continuous change, for "*Ehyeh Asher Ehyeh*" is clearly an affirmation that goes on forever: "*Ehyeh Asher Ehyeh Asher Ehyeh Asher Ehyeh. . . .*"

Then the Voice continues: "Tell Pharaoh you were sent by *Ehyeh*." All right, a nickname: The whole sentence is too cumbersome, especially if Moses realizes that its essence is an infinite repetition/transformation. "I Will Be" is utterly sufficient to get the point across.

And finally, the Voice is somehow able to speak out an impossible Name, a word that has no vowels: "*YHWH*."

I invite you to pause and try to pronounce this word, this Name. It is not "Yahweh," for it has no vowels. It is not "Jehovah," for it has no vowels.

For about the last 2,000 years, Jewish tradition has taught that we should not even try to pronounce it, but instead substitute the word "*Adonai*," which means "Lord." This teaching passed into the Greek of the Christian New Testament, where it became "*Kyrios.*" And then it passed into Latin as "*Dominus*." But in the beginning, as the flame wavered in the wind and Moses shook in awe, it was certainly not these words of domination.

What was it then? Modern grammarians have pointed out that it weaves together the letters that make up the Hebrew for the past, the present, and the future of the verb "to be." So they have suggested that it is a kind of Moebius strip of Being, time turned and twisted to come back upon itself, beyond itself: Eternal.

This is one aspect of the Name, rooted in the intellect of words, that is both profound and attractive. Better than "Lord."

But let's go back to trying to pronounce it. When I first, on the spur of the moment, decided to break the rule that said never to try pronouncing it, what came from my mouth was—*YyyyHhhhWwwwHhhh*. Breathing. Simply a breath.

And when I invited others to "pronounce" these four letters, almost everyone created the same experience: Breathing.

For me, that first moment of saying, "*YHWH*," by simply breathing—that first moment was transformative. My first thought was that this made good sense: Surely one of the real Names of the real God should not be only in Hebrew, or Egyptian, or Greek, or Latin, or Chinese, or Urdu, or Swahili, or English. It should be in all of them. And there is no sound that vibrates every human tongue except the sound of breathing.

My second thought was that it is not just human languages. Every life form on this planet breathes, and indeed we breathe each other into life. We humans, and all other animals, breathe in what the trees breathe out. The trees breathe in what we breathe out. We breathe each other into life. What could be a truer Name for God?

Let us pause for a moment. These thoughts were themselves my way of dancing in the earthquake of the world. My first, immediate response—not planned but arising in my *kishkes*, my innards, my gut—was to connect with other cultures, other religions, other languages. Surely they have a stake in what is the Name of God!

But this was not what I had been taught was Jewish wisdom. Rather, I had been taught that our relationship with *YHWH* was unique. Asking about God's Name in other languages was precisely the wrong question. Even worse than daring to pronounce the "Unpronounceable Name."

Wait! Once I ripped away the command not to pronounce the Name, the sudden reality arose: "Pronouncing" it was not just forbidden, but impossible. Unless you thought just breathing was "pronouncing." It suddenly became clear that the prohibition was against even trying to pronounce it.

Why? The point was exactly that daring to "pronounce" the Name, to breathe it, was dangerous. Pronounce the Name that could not be pronounced, and it instantly became apparent that this Name, the Breath, this Wind, this Hurricane, this Spirit was universal. The Jewish people had no patent on it. If the Name could shatter Pharaoh's power, it could endanger any domineering social structure that subjugated any people, every people. Even a structure that lorded it over the Jewish people.

How clever then—not wise, but clever—centuries later, to replace the Breathing with a word, "*Adonai*," that meant "Lord." It's convenient to borrow the controlling social symbols of the Roman Empire to control this somewhat maverick community within the Empire.

Even more appropriate when Christianity took over/was taken over by the Empire to translate "*YHWH*" with "*Kyrios*" in Greek and "*Dominus*" in Latin. If you want to dominate, name what is most sacred "Dominus."

And my second thought, I realized, was yet more dangerous. Does this Name of Interbreathing mean that not only human beings count? Does this Name mean that frogs and ferns, rabbits and redwoods, bugs and bacteria, also count? Could this Name dislodge the centrality of *Homo sapiens* and make us a thread in the great woven prayer shawl of the universe, the One, *Echad?*

Back to the biblical story. When Moses and Aaron go to Pharaoh, saying, "Let my people go!" Pharaoh says indeed what Moses had predicted: "Sez who?" Moses responds by simply breathing. Pharaoh sneers, "So that's your god? I never heard of him or her, like Isis or Osiris. Doesn't stack up against the River Nile and all the other gods of Egypt—including, of course, Me."

Moses goes to the Godwrestling people, the people *Yisrael.* He tells them their God has a new name, a Name that echoes the breath, the wind, the spirit all around them. He urges them to invoke this name to demand that Pharaoh let the people go. Pharaoh becomes furious, makes life even harder for the Hebrew-speaking slaves. The people, in their first attempt to organize Brickmakers Union Number One, crumple.

But the written text is not enough. Ancient rabbis said the Torah was not written in black ink upon white parchment but in black fire on white fire. Learn to read both fires, they said. The black ink, black fire, is the text. The white spaces between the lines and letters is white fire. In its blankness we can light up midrash. New stories, new light, new reinterpretation in every generation.

And now the blank passages of parchment flame into white fire: midrash:

> The Voice calls Moses aside once more.
>
> You told them I have a new Name, but you didn't really make it stick. You are so soft-hearted that you could not bear to insist when many of them said they were used to the old Name and would keep on using it.

> So, Moses, let me tell you clearly: the reason that your organizing failed was that it takes a new Name, a new understanding of the universe, for people to be able to reshape the world.
>
> The old Name was certainly important for its time. *El Shaddai*, "The Many-Breasted God," was fine for calling on abundance, for inspiring shepherds and farmers who needed reassurance that Mother Earth would still pour forth her milk. For Abraham and Sarah, for Isaac and Rebekah, for Jacob and his wives, the God of nourishing was nurturing. But now your people have been enslaved. They work not in the fields but to build warehouses for the food that others grow. Their lives are different, and they must search out a different Meaning if they are to make change possible.

So from this unfolding story that begins at the Burning Bush, we realize how crucial naming and renaming can be. God's Name change in the crackle of flames at the Burning Bush is crucially connected with Moses's ability to begin liberating the people from slavery.

This is a lesson for today. For we see there is an intimate connection between freeing the peoples of today, resisting the Pharaohs of today, restoring an Earth to be no longer plagued by the pyramids of power that we know today, and "renaming" God—that is, coming to a deeply new understanding of the world.

At such moments, there likely will be struggles between those who want to address God and understand the world in new frameworks, and those who are satisfied: "Give me the old-time religion; it was good enough for Grandpa, it's good enough for me."

Today, many people find some of the old ways of naming God—Lord above all, King of the Universe, Judge of the recalcitrant—no longer adequate or honest. Through these metaphors, we are defining ourselves as subjects, slaves, to a ruler whose powers we have no way to exercise or challenge. But in a generation when human beings can destroy life on this planet, can splice DNA to create species as radically new as the spider goat, can overthrow Pharaohs—all the powers we once located in a Ruler far beyond us—it no longer seems truthful to invoke such metaphors. And many women, with some men, have pointed out that the old metaphors for God are overwhelmingly and pointedly masculine, bespeaking men's spiritual experience but rarely women's.

What then? Some people have poured scorn on the whole enterprise, rejecting the God-word, perhaps identifying "biological evolution" or "the historical process" as the only sources of creativity and justice. We might say that those become new names of God. Few call them that because they seem—or their proponents claim—they are discoverable, reducible, weighable. They do not trail clouds of Mystery.

Others have renamed God as the "Infinite Thou" (Buber), "the Power that draws us toward salvation" (Kaplan), "the Wellspring of Life" (Falk), "the Ground of Being" (Tillich), perhaps "the Web of Relationship" (some feminists).

As for me, I go back to that moment of the Burning Bush, reasserted in the Narrow Space of Egypt: "*YHWH*" pronounced as "Yahhhh," the "Breath of Life, the Breathing-spirit of the world." (In Hebrew, that is *ru'akh ha'olam*, and *ru'akh* is the only Hebrew noun that can take a verb either feminine or masculine. It means "breath, wind, spirit."). We know the Name of "*Yahhhh*" when it comes as "Hallelu-Yahhhh": "Let us praise the Breath of Life."

That is the Name that awakened the Utterance at Sinai: "You are not to lift up the Name of YHWH your God for emptiness" (Exodus 20:7).

Breathe. Breathe My Name. For every breath you take, you and the frogs, you and the mulberry bushes, you and the redwoods—in every breath you say My Name. Do not say it empty-headed, empty-hearted.

We, the heirs of modern science, know with more precision than our farmer/shepherd forebears that we humans, we animals, need to breathe in the oxygen that the trees and grasses breathe out. They need to breathe in the CO_2 that we breathe out. All around our green-blue Earth, the Breath of Life, *YHWH*, is *Echad*—One.

And in this generation of your lives upon this planet, be utterly aware: The interbreathing between the animals and vegetation, the Interbreathing of Oxygen and CO_2—that breathing is in crisis. Some of you human earthlings insist on sending more CO_2 into My Name, My planetary Breath, than all Earth's vegetation can transmute to Oxygen. The build-up of CO_2 heats up my Earth far more than it, and you, can bear. What you call the climate crisis is a crisis in the Name of God.

Be awed, but not surprised. For this crisis is the Turning Point in all of human history. At last you know enough to nurture the Interbreathing of all the myriad life-forms of your planet. And at last you know enough to wreck the planet.

Do not lift up my Name for emptiness! Every one of you, be conscious that each breath you take breathes in and out My Name. And all of you together, be conscious that the Interbreathing that you share will doom, or heal, the life of all of you.

When I say to people that the climate crisis is a crisis in God's Name, they gasp. It's appropriate—a breath caught just as Earth is gasping, "I can't breathe!" And then they breathe in a new way. For suddenly the climate crisis has become both more awesome and more intimate.

And when we talk about what it means to give up "Lord" and "King" in favor of "Interbreathing Spirit," something else important happens.

People begin to get past their anger at the "Angry God," the "Angry King Who Punishes." They begin to see the Breath as interweaving Act and Consequence. Karma. Enslave human beings and Earth is plagued and plagues you—because the Breath links everybody.

As people absorb this—for many, new—way of thinking about God, many soften their rigidity against all talk of God. They can open themselves to examining what is wise and what is not, instead of bristling at the very word of "God." They don't surrender, nor do I want them to. But exploration becomes possible.

Now I want to turn to the mysterious Name I mentioned, encoded in the *Kaddish*—tinged even more with Mystery than "*YHWH*." The Kaddish is one of the most frequent prayers in Jewish life. It is used to mark transitions: the shift from one aspect of prayer to another; the conclusion of a session of learning Torah; the onset of mourning for the dead, when they die and on the anniversaries forever after.

Every Kaddish begins by naming God "*Shmei rabbah*, the Great Name." "May the Great Name be lifted higher, still more holy."

For years this puzzled me.

And then I visited the Vietnam War Memorial in Washington, DC. The Memorial is simply names: close to 60,000 names of the American dead, not even counting the million dead in Vietnam whose names Americans do not know. All those names, carved into great slabs of stone, making up one Great Name.

And what came to me was that "*shmei rabbah*, the Great Name" of the Kaddish, is the weave of all the names of all the beings, past and present and those yet to be—all the beings of the universe. Every galaxy and every quark. Every human, every frog, and every buttercup.

This understanding of the Great Name bears a family resemblance to *YHWH* as the Great Interbreathing. Both of them see God embodied in and rising from all the myriad beings of the Universe.

Just as each of us breathes our unique breath into the holy Interbreathing, each of us, the singular and individual name of each of us, lives in that One Great Name. And that one name lives within us, too. In the same way, within our body every different organ bears the DNA that speaks our personal Unity, and yet each organ has its own name, its own purpose, its own identity. Each organ has unfolded from the One where we began, and each must—in attunement with the others—celebrate its uniqueness. God forbid that my brain should strive to imitate my liver! The uniqueness of each organ, each person, each life-form, is crucial to us all. The flow of all together is crucial to each one.

What might it mean to dance with this Great Name of Interbreathing in the earthquake of our lives?

If you choose to say a blessing in the Jewish mode, in Hebrew or in any other tongue of its translation, make just two gentle changes from the conventional words. Lift up the first words of the incantation this way: "*Baruch atah Yahhhh eloheynu, ruach ha'olam*—Blessed are You, Creator God, Yahhh, Interbreathing Spirit of the universe."

Add to whatever other religious, spiritual, or cultural practices that we find life giving this affirmation of our own place in the Great Name. Set aside a time each day to weave together the names we recall from our own lives that we can weave together into the Great Name.

- Lift up the names of some beings who have been your teachers. Some may be human beings—a long-dead grumpy cousin, a wise beloved pastor, a singer of the songs you came to love. Others, a turtle sunning itself on a rock, a full moon, a stinging jellyfish, a howling dog that woke the neighborhood. Give each a name, and weave those names into your own small and local pattern of the Great Name.

- Lift up the names of some beings you have taught and changed. Weave those names as well into your own small portion of the Great Name.
- Lift up your own name. Find just the right place in your woven pattern to receive it.

Then take the whole pattern you have woven and place it in the heart of you. Your name glimmers, along with many others, in the Great Name; and the Great Name glows within you.

Set aside a time each day to meditate on the in-flow/out-flow of our Breathing. There are three brief passages of Jewish prayer that might help us remember (more on this in the next chapter):

- *Elohai nishama sheh-natah bi tehorah hi.* My God, the Breath you have given *me* is clear.

  Stand or sit quietly following the breath as *It* enters your own mouth and nose, journeys to your own lungs, is carried by your bloodstream to brain and arms, to legs and belly, genitals and skin, and back to lungs and mouth and nose to be breathed out.
- *Nishmat kol chai, tivarekh et shim-cha, Yahhhhh elo-heynu.* The Breath of all life praises Your Name, for your Name Itself whispers all life, Our God.

  Follow your Breath as you breathe it out, as it merges with the out breaths of every animal on Earth, as it enters the leaves of every plant, as its CO_2 solidifies into the living carbon of root and branch and flower and seed, and as each plant breathes out oxygen for you and every animal to inbreathe. Hear each human, each plant, each animal whisper, "OUR God."

- *Kol ha'neshama t'hallel Yah, Hallelu-YAH!* Every breathing celebrates the Breath; let us all celebrate YAH, the Interbreath!

Set aside at least one hour every week to take one act to give new life to the Interbreath of oxygen and CO_2 that keeps all life alive. Nurture a garden. Plant a tree. Write a senator. Picket the entrance to an oil company headquarters. Move your money from a bank that invests in coal mines to one that invests in windmills. Solarize your house.

What connects these approaches to the Name? They all hear the Great Name in us, among us, connecting us. One Great Name. One shared Breath.

What would it mean to lift up the Name "in emptiness," as the Ten Truths at Sinai forbid? Breathing with no awareness that each breath connects us with all life. Forgetting that my own name and the names of all those beings who taught me, loved me, rebuked me, learned from me, drew life from me are all present in the Great Name, and all bear the Great Name within them.

Having come this far, having found so much truth in hearing the Name as Breath, I began to be concerned. Was my comfort a sign that I was making this understanding of the Name, the World, into an idol? Was the Name much richer than this dimension of It?

Joy Ladin teaches that of all the Queer, shape-shifting characters in the Bible's array of stories, God is the One most beyond all boundaries and definitions: a wrestler at one moment, a king at another, a milky mother, an awesome thunderstorm, a judge, a reporter of the future. . . .

I began to think about *YHWH* in a variety of guises. Jewish mysticism teaches that the world was created in four stages:

Atzilut, pure spiritual closeness to the Divine Will—indeed, simply the Will to create in the first place; Briyah, Creativity, the outpouring of imaginations, intellectual and artistic, of what a universe might look like; Yetzirah, the Shaping of some of these imagined possibilities into relationship with each other; Asiyah, the physical Actuality.

These Four Worlds were understood to exist within the Godhead and within the world, especially but not exclusively in the human practice of the continuing process of seeking to create. In the human breath, mind, heart, hands, these would become profound prayer and meditation to connect or fuse with God, use of the intellect to imagine, heartfelt efforts through emotion and ethics to connect with others, and the actual building of physical objects and institutions to embody all this wistfulness.

What might it mean, I began to wonder, to apply this Four Worlds model to the *YHWH* Name?

At the physical level of Asiyah, it seems clear that the physical effort with lips and tongue to "pronounce" the *YHWH* indeed brings forth the metaphor of God as the Breath that interweaves all living beings. It invites me to experience my own breath as part of all breathing and all of it as sacred—to be protected and celebrated.

Applying intellect to the Name in the world of Briyah, grammarians point out that *YHWH* weaves together the past, present, and future elements of the Hebrew verb "to be." These elements twist through some reality beyond time with but one surface and one edge—a kind of Moebius strip in time. "Eternal." This way of thinking leaves me chilled with awe. Maybe it teaches me that all sacred thought and action, like a spiral, is rooted in the past and spins through "now" into the future. To reject reinterpretation of the wisdom we inherit is to lock God into the past. To lock God into only the present or the future is to erase the wisdom of the past. Midrashic reinterpretation of ancient sacred wisdom makes God Eternal by constantly outdating/updating the Divine.

At the level of Atzilut, the nearest possible to ultimate union with God, some teachers have been turning the *YHWH* around into Hei-Vav-Yod-Hei, *HWYH*, and pronouncing the "Vav" as a "v" rather than a "w." So—*Havayah*, the Hebrew word for "Existence."

What then with the world of *Yetzirah*, Relationship? For two thousand years, that aspect of the Name has leaped beyond the letters altogether into "*Adonai*," Lord. Our relationship to God was that of serfs to a Master. But now we know the Universe is ordered not by hierarchy but by the way all names, like every species, are woven ecologically into One.

My friend Rabbi Jeff Roth suggests we substitute an "Aleph" for the first letter of the Name, the letter "Yod." The Name becomes "*Ahavah*," "Love." A satisfying solution for the world of Relationship, embracing both ethics and emotion. "When peace and justice kiss," says Psalm 85:10. Yet while this does far less damage to the Name than "*Adonai*," it still requires us to leap beyond the letters that were sung or breathed or flickered in the flames at the Burning Bush and Sinai.

Maybe that's the point. Maybe at the levels of spiritual, intellectual, and physical the Name makes "sense," but at the relational level the Name is always changing, melting. In every generation, calling on us in new Voices.

Seeing the Name in at least these Four Worlds is itself an ecological way of thinking, at the Ultimate level. Even the Unity shimmers as our eyes light it up and discover the varied "aspects"—"ways of seeing"—in it, each distinct yet fitting together to make up the Unity.

I come through this journey singed and wounded. AND—still convinced that in our era when the Breath of Planet Earth is choking, coughing, "I can't breathe!" into the hot and heating furnace, it remains most important to hear that choking cough as the crisis in God's Name—in this moment, the most important version of the Name.

"*You are not to lift up the Name of YHWH your God for emptiness.*"

6

Subversive Prayer: The Leopard in the Liturgy

Leopards break into the temple and drink to the dregs what is in the sacrificial pitchers; this is repeated over and over again; finally it can be calculated in advance, and it becomes a part of the ceremony.

—Franz Kafka

I felt as if my legs were praying.

—Rabbi Abraham Joshua Heschel
(on returning from the Selma, Alabama, march demanding full voting rights for Black Americans)

The beginning of prayer is praise. The power of worship is song. To worship is to join the cosmos in praising God.

—Rabbi Abraham Joshua Heschel

> *Prayer is meaningless unless it is subversive, unless it seeks to overthrow and to ruin the pyramids of callousness, hatred, opportunism, falsehoods. The liturgical movement must become a revolutionary movement.*
>
> —Rabbi Abraham Joshua Heschel

If a new "Name of God" is a new way of understanding the world, then new forms of prayer and worship are ways of bringing one's own deepest thoughts and feelings to that new understanding of the universe.

There are two quite different ways to understand Kafka's Torah teaching. One is that the leopard is forced into the cage of liturgy and loses its power to challenge. Loses the power to subvert. The other is that the shock of interference in old forms of prayer may permanently change the paradigm—change what prayer is.

For me, the story opens up both possibilities. It all depends on what we do with the leopard. When I tell Kafka's story, I tell it this way: "One day, a leopard came stalking into the synagogue, roaring and lashing its tale. Three weeks later, it had become part of the liturgy."

People laugh—ruefully. They understand that I am saying the roaring energy of the leopard has been tamed. They yearn for that energy to be reawakened, even though they know there is some danger in it.

Then I say that I see the mission of my life work, in words or silences of prayer, and in words and silences in ancient wisdom, is to let the leopard out of the cage. For "prayer is meaningless unless it is subversive."

Heschel, great-grandson of one of the great Hassidic rebbes, knew perfectly well that legs could pray—especially through rhythmic and ecstatic dancing. But the notion that legs could pray by marching alongside a Southern Black Baptist preacher to change the laws of a secular society—that would have been at least a puzzle and at most anathema to his Hasidic forebears. As it was to his academic colleagues at the Jewish Theological Seminary!

"Subversive prayer"? A leopard roaring in the synagogue!

Would marching-as-prayer subvert the seminary's paradigm of muttered prayer in cloistered synagogues? Would it subvert the politicians' paradigm that politics was votes and money, surely not the passions of gospel shouts, Amos and Jeremiah? Or would it turn tame, perhaps a way of mobilizing thousands to uphold old "immovable" truths in the midst of God's Earthquake? Old truths about abortion and White supremacy? That way of protecting vested interests and institutions, "the forces that continue to destroy the promise, the hope, the vision" would be the opposite of "subversive."

Since Heschel fifty years ago, two great subversions have erupted in the religious communities I know—one in what "prayer" is, and one in what it is for, how it is directed. The change in what prayer is, is that there have been efforts to infuse it with far more bodily awareness. The change in how it is directed is that our awareness of a great crisis in the Great Earth Body, in relations between adamah and adam, Earth and human earthling, are directing prayer toward words that are more conscious of the crisis. If the entire future existence of the human race and of the web of life in which it grew is at stake, there could hardly be a more urgent need for the deep awareness that prayer is supposed to be.

The growing desire to focus on this crisis in and with all Earth, and the urge toward more embodied prayer, hark back to ancient Temple Judaism. In biblical Judaism, connection with God was chiefly through bodily connection with Earth. Israelites brought food (beef, mutton, grain, bread, pancakes, fruit, wine, water) and branches of trees to the Temple to be offered by priests chosen by their bodies (hereditarily, and only by those with "unblemished" bodies), by burning, waving, or pouring these earthy elements for the Breath of Life.

With the end of Temple Judaism and the onset of Rabbinic Judaism came a great shift: People got in touch with God chiefly through words—prayer and Torah study. The Rabbis—leaders and teachers of doing this—were chosen according to their adeptness in the serious and playful use of words, not according to the ancestry of their bodies.

So especially for the Judaism of the last two thousand years, focused away from Earth, these shifts toward more embodied and Earth-oriented prayer offer great challenges and openings of Spirit. New forms are emerging that may be reminiscent of but not the same as the embodied offerings of three thousand years ago.

Let us glance at some of the newly emerging streams of more embodied prayer.

Meditation

The infusion of silent meditation, often learned from Buddhist teachers, into Jewish and Christian prayer. Sometimes this has meant not just infusions but the replacement with meditation of what those traditions knew as prayer. Silent meditation has encouraged many of its practitioners to be far more aware of their own bodies and of the body of Earth in which they sit and walk. It has invited God as Breath, the YyyyHhhhWwww Hhhh, into the very warp and woof of "prayer," rather than only as another "word" in the words of prayer.

This practice can be "subversive" not only in toppling whole structures of traditional prayer, but in teaching that silence, breathing, and focusing on love for all the world can be valid expressions of God connection that reach beyond the specific ethnic religious community where they may be practiced.

Chant

Traditional Jewish prayer has been unfolded and enriched with new words of poetry and song for at least the last two thousand years. Since no generation wants to throw out the treasures of the past or to allow the treasures of its own to be forgotten, prayer services have gotten longer and longer. For some, these thousands of words clog the pipeline to God. One response has been the creation of "chanting services" that may focus on just ten chants of five or six words each from traditional sources like the Psalms. Each chant becomes a well of Spirit to be plumbed in depth, rather than thin ice to speedily skate across. Communal chanting becomes a way of communal breathing, giving focus and pattern to the Breath.

Dance

If in our generation we seek a synthesis between the body/Earth focus of ancient Judaism and the word focus of Rabbinic Judaism, perhaps that synthesis comes in the form of sacred dance, filling movements of the body with conscious meaning as if the whole body, not the mouth alone, were praying. There have been growing numbers of experiments in creating such improvisational liturgical dance, expressing prayerfulness in the moment.

The Kohenet Movement: Hebrew Priestesses

Two of the strongest impulses to "subvert" conventional prayer in order to subvert conventional forces of oppression—the emergence of women's energy and the reemergence of earthy celebration—have come together in the movement to create and train a new guild of spiritual leaders, distinct from the rabbinate: the Hebrew priestess. The name alone signals its "subversive" intent, evoking memories of ancient charges by male Prophets that Hebrew women were celebrating goddesses. Jeremiah, for example (7:18), charges that women were baking cookies to celebrate the "Queen of Heaven" (perhaps croissants to honor the crescent Moon?).

The Kohenet movement is not worshipping gods other than the One; it is experiencing the One in wind and rain and rocks, making labyrinths to invoke the energy of the One by walking on a patterned Earth, tasting the arts of cookery as channels for spiritual expression. Jewish ritual already has similar elements, like waving a bundle of branches and fruit in the seven directions of the world during the harvest festival of Sukkot, eating Matzah and a Bitter Herb as crucial ways of remembering slavery and celebrating freedom. Where the Kohenet movement differs is in making Earth and women central, the Talmud and other rabbinic wordplay much less important.

Earth-Oriented Words and Symbols of Formal Communal Prayer

Some religious communities are bringing their prayer and practice to bear on the radical dangers posed by the climate crisis to the web of human and more-than-human life-forms on Planet Earth.

There are two aspects of what is beginning to happen in relating prayer to the present crisis of our planet. One is exploring how Earth awareness can enter more deeply into our formal prayer services. The other is exploring how public action intended to affect public and corporate policy toward the Earth can become prayerful.

Earth Awareness in Formal Prayer

One powerful way to enhance earth awareness in the formal prayer of many religious traditions would be to introduce new symbols and rituals into them. One extraordinarily powerful effort along these lines was undertaken at the "Interfaith Summit on the Climate Crisis" called in 2008 by the Church of Sweden and chaired by its archbishop in Uppsala. The initial service in the Cathedral of Uppsala was in many ways a conventional interfaith service: *shofar* (ram's horn) blown by Jews, a bell rung by Buddhists, etc. The most moving aspect of the initial service was the rolling of a large green (moss) globe down the center aisle of the cathedral—the symbol of no one religious community and the possible symbol for them all.

A version of this practice has been introduced since then into a number of multireligious services focusing on the climate crisis—especially several held by Interfaith Moral Action on Climate at the White House fence and Lafayette Park in 2012 and 2013, and at Lincoln Square in New York City in 2016.

At those events, the participants passed an inflatable Globe from hand to hand, singing the following familiar song:

We have the whole world in our hands,
We have the rain and the forests in our hands,
We have the wind and the willows in our hands,
WE HAVE THE WHOLE WORLD IN OUR HANDS!

We have the rivers and the mountains in our hands,
We have the lakes and the oceans in our hands
We have you and me in our hands,
WE HAVE THE WHOLE WORLD IN OUR HANDS.

We have the trees and the tigers in our hands,
We have our sisters and our brothers in our hands,
We have our children and *their* children in our hands,
WE HAVE THE WHOLE WORLD IN OUR HANDS!

It is both factually and theologically notable that this liturgy transformed an older hymn in which the refrain was, "*He* has the whole world in *His* hands."

That assertion—*He* is in charge of the world—is closely related to a major traditional metaphor in most Jewish,

Christian, and Muslim prayer. In that metaphor, God is King, Lord, Judge—above and beyond the human beings who are praying. In regard to the Earth, this metaphor crowned a series of hierarchies:

The great Chain of Being is a hierarchy from rocks and rivers up to vegetation, thence up to animals, then to human beings and finally up to the Divine King and Lord.

Today we know that the relationship between the human species and the Earth is ill described by these metaphors of hierarchy. Not only do we know that what we breathe in depends upon what the trees and grasses breathe out; now we know that within our own guts are myriads of microscopic creatures that occasionally make us sick but far more often keep us alive and healthy. What's more, they have a strong impact on how our brains work. Who is in charge here? Who is "me" here?

There is no "environment" in the sense of an "environs" that is "out there," not us. There are fringes, not fences, between us and other life, and sometimes not even fringes at our edges but in our very innards.

Though now we know the Human species has indeed great power to shape and damage the web of life on Earth, we also know today that we are part of that web—a strand within it—not simply above and beyond it. What we may do to the web out of our unusual power also has an impact upon us. The more we act as if we are in total control, the closer we come to "totaling" the whole intricate process (to use a phrase that—perhaps not accidentally—comes from the world of automobiles).

So those metaphors of ordered hierarchy are no longer truthful, viable, or useful to us as tools of spiritual enlightenment.

If we are to seek spiritual depth and height, the whole framework of prayer must be transformed.

The metaphor that God is the Interbreathing of all life is far more truthful than the metaphor that God is King and

Lord. It brings together spiritual truth and scientific fact. It has only been about 250 years since human beings discovered that the great exchange of carbon dioxide and oxygen between plants and animals is what keeps our planet alive. Yet this scientific fact echoes the ancient sense that we are all interwoven, interbreathing.

Even to say the word "spiritual" is to teach the importance of this interbreathing. For just as the word "*spiritus*" in Latin means "breath" and "wind" as well as what we call "spirit," so the word "*ruach*" in Hebrew means "breath," "wind," and "spirit." Much the same sense is expressed in many other languages.

Breathing Sounds

What would it mean, then, to reframe our forms of prayer around the metaphor of God as interbreathing? I will speak here from my own roots in Jewish prayer, but the basic question should arise in the prayers of all cultures. One way of reaffirming Breath is treating the sound and rhythm of prayer as important as the intellectual meaning of the words. For example, the Hebrew prayer that affirms our radical amazement at experiencing the world is filled with the vowel of "O!" while the prayer just after it, celebrating God's love, is filled with the vowel of "Ah!" The central affirmation of Jewish prayer, asserting the Unity of God, begins with the Hebrew word "*Sh'ma*," which means "Hear!" or "Listen!" It is organically connected, therefore, that the word begins with "Sh'sh'sh."

Drawing on our new attention to the Breath, we might hear the Sh'ma saying "*Hush'sh'sh* and listen, you Godwrestlers! Our God is the Interbreathing of all life, and the interbreathing is ONE."

In the traditional Jewish prayer book, the Sh'ma is followed by three paragraphs of explication and affirmation. The second paragraph is especially devoted to the relationship between human beings and the earth. It asserts that if human beings follow the sacred teachings that indeed the Divine is One, then the rivers will run, the rains will fall, the heavens will bless the earth, and the earth will be abundantly fruitful in feeding human beings, in making the harvest abundant, and in making the land flourish.

But the paragraph continues that if we follow false gods, if we carve the world up into parts and worship not the One Breath of life but some substitute piece we have carved out—then the rivers won't run, the rain won't fall, and the Heavens will become our enemy. We will perish from the good Earth that the One Breath of life, our God, has given us.

In the last half-century, that second paragraph has been excised from many modern Jewish prayer books. The argument for removing it has been that it teaches a false notion of reward coming for sure from good action and punishment coming from bad action. But that excision came before we understood how interwoven, how fragile is our relationship with the Earth, and how we might in fact act with such strength and arrogance as to wound even the rain and the rivers. So as a way of understanding the Sh'ma so that Earth really matters in our present generation, I offer this interpretive translation of the three paragraphs that can be chanted quite easily in English:

Sh'ma for the 21st Century: A Jewish Invocation of the Unity

All together chant, "*Sh'ma Yisrael Yahhh eloheynu Yahhhh echad.*" In English, "Hush, Hush and Hear, You Godwrestlers: The Breath of Life is your God; the Breath of Life is ONE."

[Then, going around the room, each person reads one stanza:]

Sh'sh'sh'ma Yisra'el—
Hush'sh'sh and Listen, You Godwrestlers—
Pause from your wrestling and hush'sh'sh

To hear—*YyyyHhhhWwwwHhhh / Yahhhh.*
Hear in the stillness the still silent voice,
The silent breathing that intertwines life;
YyyyHhhhWwwwHhhh / Yahhhh eloheynu

Breath of life is our God,
Uniting all varied
forces creating
all worlds into one-ness,
Each breath unique,
And all unified;
Listen, You Godwrestlers—
No one people alone
owns this Unify-force;
YyyyHhhhWwwwHhhh / Yahh is ONE.

If you hush and then listen,
yes hush and then listen
to the teachings of YHWH/Yahh,
the One Breath of Life,
that the world is One—
If you hear in the stillness the still silent voice,
The silent breathing that intertwines life—

If we Breathe in the quiet,
Interbreathe with all Life—
Still small Voice of us all—
We will feel the Connections;
We will make the connections
and the rain will fall rightly
The grains will grow rightly
The rivers will run,
The heavens will smile,

The forests will flourish,
The good earth will fruitfully feed us,
And all life weave the future in fullness.
Earthlings / good Earth.
But if we break the One Breath into pieces
And erect into idols these pieces of Truth,
If we choose these mere pieces to worship:
gods of race or of nation
gods of wealth and of power,
gods of greed and addiction—
Big Oil or Big Coal—
If we Do and we Make and Produce without Pausing to Be;
If we heat the One Breath with our burnings—
Then the Breath will flare up into scorching;
Great ice fields will melt
And great storms will erupt:
Floods will drown our homes and our cities.

The rain will not fall—
or will turn to sharp acid—
The rivers won't run—
or flood homes and cities;
The corn will parch in the field,
The poor will find little to eat,
The heavens themselves
will take arms against us:
the ozone will fail us,
the oil that we burn
will scorch our whole planet.
Then each nation will come
to the gates of its cities,
Trembling in fear
Where their own culture ends,
and another begins,

Compassion will vanish
And each people will snarl—
"Here we speak the same language
"But out there is bar-bar-barbaric,
"They may kill without speaking—"
And no one will help.

The Breath, Holy Wind, Holy Spirit
Will become Hurricanes of Disaster
and from the good earth
that the Breath of Life gives us,
We will vanish;
yes, perish.
What must we do?

On the edges of each Self
take care to weave fringes,
threads of connection.
So we end not with sharpness,
A fence or a wall,
But with sacred mixing
of cloth and of air—
A fringe that is fuzzy,
part ours and part God's:
They bind us together,
Make One from our one-ness.
Good fringes / good neighbors.
At the gates of our cities,
where our own culture ends,
and another begins,
We must pause in the gateway to write on its walls
And to chant in its passage:
"Each gate is unique in the world that is One."
Connect what we see with our eyes

To what we do with our hands.
If we see that a day is coming
That will burn like a furnace—
Turn for our healing to a sun of justice,
To its wings of wind and its rays of light
To empower all peoples.

Deep mirrors / true seeing.
Time loving / right action.
The Infinite / One.

Then the rains will fall
Time by time, time by time;
The rivers will run,
The heavens will smile,
The grass will grow,
The forests will flourish,
The good earth will fruitfully feed us,
And all life weave the future in fullness.
[*ALL SAY IN UNISON*]
Honor the web that all of us weave.
Breathe together the Breath of all Life.

[*The community simply breathes quietly for a few minutes, staying aware that each breath comes from all breath.*]

There is part of the traditional Jewish morning prayer service that actually focuses on Breath. There are three passages in which the Hebrew word *neshama* (breath) is central.

The first begins *Elohai neshamahh sheh-natahhh bi t'horahhh hi*; in English, "The breath *my* God has placed within *me* is clear." In that prayer, many of the words that follow are also structured to end in a deliberately long drawn-out "*ahhhh*" sound, making the prayer that is intellectually about breath into itself a breathing exercise.

The second says, *Nishmat kol chai tivarekh et shim-cha, Yahhhh eloheynu*; in English, "The breath of all life blesses your Name, *our* God. Thus, as in the "O!" sound of radical amazement, the medium and the message cohere.

The third Breath prayer says, *Kol ha'neshamah t'hallel YAH—Hallelu-Yahhhh!*; that is, in English, "*Every* breath praises Yah, the breath of life."

In order to pray with our bodies so that Earth's body really matters, we might actually breathe these three different passages in three different ways.

For the first, we might experience the breath coming into our noses, mouths, and throats; moving into our lungs to be picked up by our bloodstream; bearing the oxygen to our brain, our arms, our heart and legs, and genitals and skin—to all our organs that through their diversity make each of us into a One. This is *my* breath, and it comes from *my* God.

The second passage invites us to see the breath of all life, praising the name of *our* God—no longer *my* God but our God. Whose "*our*"? Not Jews alone or human beings alone, but all life-forms, rejoicing in *our* God. For this passage, we might begin by experiencing how our breath—now mostly carbon dioxide—leaves our mouths and noses; how it moves into the air and atmosphere of all God's creatures; how it moves into a plant and is breathed in by trees and grasses; how they absorb the carbon to make new leaves, new wood—and then breathe out oxygen into the world, so that we can breathe it in.

We might chant the passage thus:

Nishmat

You Whose very Name—
YyyyHhhhWwwwHhhh—
Is the Breath of Life,
The breathing of all life

Gives joy and blessing to Your Name.
As lovers lie within each other's arms,
Whispering each the other's name
Into the other's ear,
So we lie in Your arms,
Breathing with each breath
Your Name, Your Truth, Your Unity.
You alone,
Your Breath of Life alone,
Guides us,
Frees us,
Transforms us,
Heals us,
Nurtures us,
Teaches us.
First, last,
Future, past,
Inward, outward,
Beyond, between,
You are the breathing that gives life to all the worlds.
And we do the breathing that gives life to all the worlds.
As we breathe in what the trees breathe out,
And the trees breathe in what we breathe out,
So we breathe each other into life,
We and You.
YyyyHhhhWwwwHhhh.

And finally, the third passage comes from the very end phrase of Psalm 150, the last Psalm. It affirms that every breath praises, blesses, the God who is the breath of life. It uses one of the ancient names of God—Yah, as in Hallelu-Yah—the name that has the initial Y and the ending H of the *YHWH* Name. You might say it is an intimate nickname of *YHWH*.

The exercise I have described is a way of teaching and reminding the community that it is part of Earth, interwoven with Earth, not its ruler nor the Viceroy of a King still higher and more Royal.

With this new relationship with Earth in mind, we can move to the moment in the Jewish service that affirms there is a *minyan*, a community, a quorum for prayer, in the room. Traditionally, this required ten male Jews at least thirteen years and one day old. Now ten adult Jews of any gender would, in many Jewish circles, make a minyan.

As we pause to say a welcoming affirmation—*Let us praise that holy breath of life which is indeed to be well praised*—we might in our new mode look from face to face around the room. We call to mind the teaching that each face is unique because God's Face is so varied. We call to mind the teaching that we must fit together to affirm each Self in the web of God's Image. We pause at each face to say in our hearts, "*This* is the Face of God. And *this*, so different, is the Face of God. And this, and this, and this."

We affirm that each face—so different not only in its physical shape and look but in its history and future—is the Face of God, not despite their differences but precisely because of their diversity. For the Infinite can only be expressed in the world through the many facets of diversity.

With Earth in mind, we might then turn to see the green Faces of God—especially if the prayer space has been so shaped that there are windows to see the trees and grasses. (For this kind of prayer, indeed it would be important for the spaces of our congregations to include exactly these kinds of windows.)

Someone might actually say, "We invite into our minyan these green faces of the holy Breath of life, for no minyan could live and breathe if these green faces of the Holy One were not breathing into us what we need to live."

There are other moments in the service when this old/new metaphor seems more fitting than "King" or "Lord." For example, as we celebrate the way in which the Red Sea was blown apart for the Israelites to walk through into freedom, the action of a great "Wind," the wind of change, seems a more fitting metaphor for the force that compelled the sea to split than the metaphor of "King."

And in the Aleynu prayer where traditionally we bow and bend before the Royal Majesty, we can indeed bow and bend and let our bodies wave and move in the great Wind of change. As the Shaker community of ecstatic mystics sang (and danced),

'Tis the gift to be simple, 'tis the gift to be free
'Tis the gift to come down where we ought to be,
And when we find ourselves in the place just right,
'Twill be in the valley of love and delight.
When true simplicity is gained,
To bow and to bend we will not be ashamed.
To turn, turn, will be our delight—
Till by turning, turning we come 'round right!

To that song we might add a second verse:

'Tis a gift to be urgent, 'tis a gift to be true,
'Tis a gift to rise up as we yearn to do;
When we breathe together to shape a world of right,
We'll regrow the Garden of love and delight.
When winds of justice are once again unchained
To bend in those breezes we shall not be ashamed,
Turning, turning will be our delight,
Till by turning, turning we come 'round right.

Finally, the Kaddish that appears as a bridge between sections of Jewish prayer addresses God as "*shmei rabbah*," the Great

Name. One way to understand the "Great Name" is that it is the Name that includes all the names of all the beings in the world—every galaxy and every quark, each distinctive species, all mountains, rocks, and rivers (as the nearly sixty thousand names in the Vietnam War Memorial in Washington, DC, make up one "great name"). Asking people to envision and weave together several of these names that have moved and changed them would help the whole community to begin weaving these names into the Great Name, and thus heighten awareness of how all Earth is interwoven.

Dialogical Davvening

All these efforts look toward engaging those who pray much more fully in the meaning of prayerful connection to God in their own lives. Another way of doing this is "dialogical davvening (prayer)," inviting those who pray into an I–Thou experience with each other.

In this approach, pairs of people within the congregation face each other, with the text of a psalm in their hands. One begins by reciting a line of the psalm, and then adds a self-created line that emerges in the moment, expressing the feeling or thought this line evokes. The other partner then responds by reciting the next line with a special attention and response to the partner's comment, and so on through the psalm.

This process makes the psalm into the grounding of a real relationship with the Other, and thus with the infinite, eternal I–Thou, which was Martin Buber's understanding of God. The people enter the psalm and let the psalm enter them. In this way the aloofness of the ancient sacred word is softened so that its power to control them from afar is subverted into its ability to help them transform themselves.

Lighting Lights, the Inner and the Outer

In traditional Jewish practice, every Shabbat begins and ends with the lighting of candles, originally to mark our decision that during Shabbat we would NOT light fires and thus disturb the balance of the universe. That was part of a broader sense that on Shabbat we would minimize "making" and "doing" in honor of "being." Lighting candles marks every festival as well, and for Hanukkah, during the darkest time of year, we mix the darkness with lights, affirming both Clarity and Mystery. All these practices point us toward the roots of festivity and joy in the dance of Earth, Moon, and Sun.

All the festivals are ultimately born from that supernal Dance, and in our era when the Dance itself is in danger, our Mother Earth needs the help of her festival children to heal from the wounds she is suffering. From the standpoint of Humanity, we can share communal "festive" joy by joining in practices and awarenesses that make the earthiness explicit.

We might, for instance, do that with Light itself by reciting together this fiery focus before lighting the candles of our spiritual practice:

Between the Fires

We are the generations
that stand between the fires.
Behind us the fire and smoke
that rose from Auschwitz and from Hiroshima,
Not yet behind us the burning forests of the Amazon,
torched for the sake of fast hamburger.
Not yet behind us the hottest years of human history
that bring upon us—
Melted ice fields. Flooded cities.
Scorching droughts. Murderous wildfires.

Before us we among all life-forms
face the nightmare of a Flood of Fire,
the heat and smoke that could consume all Earth.

To douse that outer all-consuming fire
We must light again in our own hearts
the inner fire of love and liberation
that burned in the Burning Bush.
The fire that did not consume the Bush or Earth it burned in,
the Fire that can never be extinguished,
The fire in the heart of every community and all Creation.
It is our task to make from inner fire
Not an all-consuming blaze
But the light in which we see more clearly
The Rainbow Covenant glowing
in the many-colored faces of all life.

Making Public Advocacy Actions Prayerful

Can "praying with our legs," like Heschel, be even more imbued with spiritual symbols and energy that, like many actions of the Freedom Movement in the South during the 1960s, draw truly and authentically on the Spirit, deepen commitment, and broaden support?

The intertwined religious stories of Passover and Holy Week speak in powerful ways to the danger facing the Earth—and in Islam, though there is no analogous festival, the Exodus story and the story of Jesus are major aspects of the Qu'ran. So interfaith and multireligious groups have drawn on this tradition in these ways:

- Recalling that the arrogance and stubbornness of Pharaoh brought plagues upon the Earth—all of them ecological disasters—as well as oppression upon the human community.
- Understanding the yearly gatherings of a million people in ancient Jerusalem on Passover itself and the march of protest against the Roman Empire led by

Jesus at Passover time on the first Palm Sunday—a march to protest against oppression by the Pharaohs and Caesars of that and every generation.

- Holding public religious gatherings to lift up the symbols of Passover and Palm Sunday—matzah and palms—in calls to act against the plagues of global scorching brought on by the modern Corporate Carbon Pharaohs of Big Coal and Oil.
- Marking the matzah as a call to urgent action—what Dr. Martin Luther King called "the fierce urgency of Now"—and the palms as witnesses of fresh green life renewed.
- Carrying these religious celebrations into the city streets with marches interspersed with vigils at local centers of "pyramidal power."
- Welcoming arrests at the White House and other power centers to demand urgent action against Tar Sands pipelines, coal-plant CO_2 emissions, and so on.

Actions that draw on these themes were carried out at the White House in 2014, in Manhattan on Palm Sunday, marches followed by a Freedom Seder at Judson Memorial Church in 2010, and street theater against the Carbon Pharaohs at the Koch Theater in Lincoln Center in Manhattan in 2016.

Activists of varied faith traditions, as well as secular activists, have in similar ways reconfigured many Jewish and Christian festivals as direct actions to protect and heal the Earth:

- Reshaping Tu B'Shvat, the Jewish festival of ReBirthday of the Trees, as a time for protests and civil disobedience to protect ancient redwoods and the Everglades from corporate depredation.
- Drawing on the tradition of Hanukkah as celebrating the miraculous fulfillment of one day's supply of sacred oil to meet eight days' needs as a spur to energy conservation.

- Celebrating Hoshana Rabbah, the seventh day of the harvest festival of Sukkot, a day traditionally set aside for invoking rain, honoring the seven days of Creation, and praying for salvation from insect swarms, droughts, and other natural disasters—as a day of protest on the shores of the Hudson River in Beacon, NY, against the corporate poisoning of the Hudson River with PCBs.
- Observing the laments of Tisha B'Av over the destruction of the ancient Holy Temples in Jerusalem by two Empires—Babylon and Rome—by defining the universal Temple of today as Earth itself, and gathering at the US Capitol in the midst of the spring and summer of 2010 to lament the ongoing destruction of Temple Earth, and demand action to save it from the Carbon Pharaohs aching to destroy it.

The reframing of Jewish fasts and festivals in this way has been especially attractive because the Jewish festival cycle is closely keyed to the dance of Sun, Moon, and Earth. Many of the festivals, therefore, can be understood as universal at heart though clothed in Jewish history and culture. Probably for that reason, these actions drawing on uniquely Jewish ceremonies and practices have often attracted members of other faith traditions and secular ecoactivists to take part.

As the experience of religious communities grows in exploring this whole area of reframing festivals as forms of public action, there has begun to emerge a pattern of spiritual practice in each event: first, public celebration of Earth; then, mourning for its wounds and dangers; finally, a commitment and covenant to act on its behalf and to challenge whatever power centers are worsening its wounds.

This threefold pattern echoes many powerful evocations of spiritual depth: prosperity of ancient Israel in Egypt, slavery, and Exodus; the Promised Land, Exile, and Return; Celebration, Crucifixion, Resurrection; Gautama's life of royal luxury, his discovery of suffering, Enlightenment.

This process of reframing festival observances as action to protect the Earth has only begun. It is likely that much more richness of spiritual imagination and political adeptness will be brought to bear as religious and spiritual communities keep facing the planetary crisis.

And what about the deepest festival of all—Shabbat? It is a reflection and celebration of the cosmic truth that there is a rhythm of Doing and Being, Work and Rest—cosmic, not limited to any people, any life-form. And in the same Breath, it is a reflection and celebration of the joyful need that all humanity needs this same rhythm, beyond ethnicity and class. Is there a way of practicing Shabbat that both within itself carries out the restful rhythm, and reaches out beyond itself, "seeking to overthrow the forces that continue to destroy the promise, the hope, the vision"?

Can we imagine carrying Shabbat into public space in chanting vigils, silent sit-downs, "to overthrow the pyramids of callousness and hatred," to challenge the Pharaohs that force and seduce us, adam and adamah, into still More and More and More and More, violating cosmos and subjugating life?

In great crises of previous world history, institutions of overreach and overkill that take previous conventions of limited arrogance and cruelty beyond those limits have called into being waves of new forms of protest, compassion, and community. All these explorations we have described point to new ways of embodying prayer and, often, interweaving different religious traditions. Breathing the Breath transcends our every language. Do these experiments point toward the emergence of new communities that dissolve and reweave the communities we have known the last few thousand years? Will it be new communities that come alive to dance in God's earthquake?

7

God's Image in the Human Jigsaw Puzzle

Creator God said, "Let us make humankind in Our image, according to Our likeness!" . . . God created humankind in God's image, in the image of God did The One create it. Male and female did The One create them.

—Genesis 1:24, 26

What is the relationship between individual human beings and the communities they live in? Is one of them the irreducible heart of human existence? Which? Is one the great fountain of joy for human beings, and the other, the source of great dangers of physical and ethical disaster? Which?

These issues are some of the sharpest in our society today. Do we focus on the politics of "identity" (read "community")? Are "human rights" totally individual, not colored by community membership or history—so that a "color-blind Constitution" means we must pay no attention to the present impacts of past slavery, or to the possible benefits of being honored as one in a long line of Harvard alumni or a long line of Irish cops?

In a traditional Jewish prayer service, there is actually a moment that stands at the knife edge of this question. When the service begins, each prayer is understood to be coming from each pray-er as an individual. Then there is a prayer recited in the plural—"Let *us* bless YHWH/Yahhh/The Breath of Life" and the entire congregation responds. The individuals have become a community.

In some congregations, just before the plural prayer, members of the congregation pause to look from face to face, lifting up a teaching from the Bible and the Talmud.

As we have just seen, the Bible asserts that each human being is made in the Image of God.

And the rabbis of the Talmud asked, What does this mean?

> Our Rabbis taught: Adam, the first human being, was created as a single person to show forth the greatness of the Ruler Who is beyond all rulers, the Blessed Holy One. For if a human ruler [like Caesar, the Roman Emperor] mints many coins from one mold, they all carry the same image, they all look the same. But the Blessed Holy One shaped all human beings in the Divine Image, as Adam was shaped in the Divine Image [Genesis 1:27], "*b'tzelem elohim*, in the Image of God." And yet not one of them resembles another.
>
> —Sanhedrin 38a; Soncino transl., 240

This seems a strong assertion of the primacy of the individual. "Not one of them resembles another" is God's Own doing.

But wait. They are all different from each other, yet each is shaped in a single Image, the Image of the One. Does that mean we do resemble each other? How?

As the congregants look around the circle at each other, they pause at each face and say, silently, "This face is the Face of God!" And then, "*This* face, and *this*, and *this*—so different, not only in physical shape and expression but in the past and future of each face, is the Face of God!"

Remarkably, the Talmud is making a political statement and a spiritual statement in the very same breath. The rabbis were living under the heel of the Roman Empire. Surely Rome was all powerful. To be a Jew meant being trampled under Caesar's legions, threatened with torture and execution, watching thousands on the Roman cross—or becoming one of them! Did this exhaust the meaning of existence—to be either an oppressor or oppressed?

Yet what seemed the power of Caesar to dominate—he could make all his coins, the economy, the entire society, resemble him—was false; he could not create creativity.

The very diversity of human faces shows forth the Unity and Infinity of God, whereas the uniformity of imperial coins makes clear the limitations on the power of an emperor.

Again, an issue that dovetails with some of the questions we face today, as would-be despots emerge from social crisis. Are there resources of the Spirit that are able to mount a "political" challenge to them?

The Talmud's teaching casts light on one of the best-known Gospel stories of Jesus's life—and for centuries one that has most puzzled his followers as those stories crystallized into what became Christianity. It is the tale of an encounter concerning the image on a coin.

The story appears in Matthew 22:15–22, Mark 12:13–17, and Luke 20:19–26. It is almost the same in all three places.

According to the story, some of Jesus's opponents among the Pharisees sent people to trick Jesus into saying something that would provide a pretext for his arrest.

Wait. Let us take note that even before we hear the rest of the story, already this reference to "the Pharisees" raises some interesting interreligious problems. Who were they?

As different groups of Jews struggled to work out their different responses to the turmoil created by Roman-Hellenistic domination, the Pharisees' way of reforming and reinterpreting Torah crystallized into Rabbinic Judaism. In general, the Pharisees sided with the poor against the Roman occupation and its allies in the Jewish "establishment."

Some scholars today think that during his own lifetime Jesus may have seen himself as one of or closely akin to the Pharisees, among their "radical" wing. In that case, "the Pharisees" as a body would not have been his opponents but some among them would have. The relationship might have been more like that between Father Dan Berrigan and "the Catholic priesthood." Berrigan was a priest, not an opponent of "the priests." Yet clearly he was a radical among them.

As the Gospels emerged from oral memory into written histories, the separation between those Jews who chose Christianity and those who chose the rabbinic path became sharper, and it became easier for Christians to see the Pharisees as "Other."

Back to the story.

One of these Pharisees spoke up, saying, "Rabbi, we know that what you speak and teach is sound; you pay deference to no one, but teach in all honesty the life-path that God requires. Give us your ruling on this: Are we or are we not permitted to pay taxes to the Roman Emperor?"

Jesus, say the Gospels, saw through their trick and said to them, "Show me a silver coin." When they dug one out for him, no doubt annoyed at his changing the subject, he asked them: "Whose image is on this coin, and whose inscription?"

Let us pause again for a moment. What was the "trick"? The coin had Caesar's image on it, with the inscription "*Divus*"—"God." To the Jews, treating an emperor as a god was idolatry. So just using the coin itself might constitute idolatry in Jewish law, and thus be forbidden. To use the coin to pay taxes to this same Caesar—still worse! But by Roman law the taxes must be paid.

So the "trick" was that by answering one way, Jesus would break Jewish law; by answering the other way, he would break Roman law. Either way, he would be subject to arrest.

But Jesus had not quite answered. Instead, he had answered the question with a question: "Whose image is on this coin, and whose inscription?" (Says the folklore, this is an old Jewish habit. As it is taught, "Why does a Jew answer a question with a question?" Answer, "Why not?")

According to Matthew, Mark, and Luke, the man who had challenged him answered, "Caesar's!"

And then Jesus did respond: "So give to Caesar what is Caesar's, and to God what is God's!"

This answer, say Matthew, Mark, and Luke, took his opponents by surprise, and they went away and left him alone.

But for two thousand years, Christians have argued over what this answer meant. What is Caesar's, and what is God's? Does the answer suggest two different spheres of life, one ruled by Caesar and one by God? Does it mean to submit to Caesar's authority in the material world, while adhering to God in the spiritual world? How do we discern the boundary?

Why did the questioners go away? Was it simply because Jesus had avoided the horns of the dilemma they had brought, and so could not be arrested for his answer?

Or was there a deeper meaning to the answer? Is the answer simply a koan, an answer that forces the questioner to seek a deeper question or break through into enlightenment?

Now let us reconnect, alongside this Gospel story, the passage we have lifted up from the Talmud. The Talmud comes from a period of historical time that overlaps the New Testament. It is thousands of pages long, because it records the teachings of thousands of rabbis who lived thousands of miles apart, some in Babylonia and some in the Land of Israel, during a period of five hundred years. It compiles their debates and dialogues, their puns and parables, their philosophic explorations and practical decisions from about the beginning of the Common Era to about 500 CE. It is a flowering of the tree that had its roots in those same Pharisees who included Jesus and who accosted Jesus, and who called him rabbi.

Now reread the story of Jesus with a single line and gesture added:

"Whose image is on this coin?" asks Jesus.

His questioner answers, "Caesar's!" Then Jesus puts his arm on the troublemaker's shoulder and asks, "And whose image is on *this* coin?"

Perhaps the troublemaker mutters an answer; perhaps he does not need to. Not till after this exchange does Jesus say, "Give to Caesar what is Caesar's and to God what is God's."

Now there is a deeper meaning to the response, and to the troublemaker's exit. Jesus has not just avoided the question and evaded the dilemma: he has answered, in a way that is much more radical than if he had said either "pay the tax" or "don't pay the tax"—a way that is profoundly radical but gives no obvious reason for arrest.

Jesus has not proposed dividing up the turf between the material and the spiritual. He has redefined the issue: Give your whole self to the One Who has imprinted Divinity upon you! You—you who are one of the Rabbis, my brother Rabbi—you know that is the point of this story! All I have done is to remind you!

The coin of the realm will matter very little, if the troublemaker listens.

So the questioner walks away, suddenly profoundly troubled by the life question that he faces.

We might ask, why does the line I have inserted not appear in the three versions of the story that we have?

It is possible that the line was censored out, as Christian tradition faced both the threats of an Empire to shatter this religion and the invitation of an Empire to become the Established Church.

Or it is possible that Jesus never needed to say the words, because his "Pharisee" questioners understood the point perfectly well. After all, on the basis of the passage in the Talmud, we can be fairly certain that the teaching comparing God's Image upon Adam to Caesar's image on the coinage was already well known among the rabbis.

For me, this reading of the two passages—one from Talmud, one from the New Testament—brings with it two levels of greater wholeness, deeper meaning.

The first level is that each of the two passages enriches the meaning of the other. Read together, they fuse the spiritual and the political, instead of splitting the world into two domains. But they fuse the two from the bottom up, not by Caesar's top-down idolatry.

In this reading, the claim of the Divine Ruler to rule over an emperor includes and subverts the political realm, because each individual human being is far more God than is the Imperial "Divus" on the official coin. God can create infinite diversity and eternal renewal and so is far richer than the imperial treasury—which can create only uniformity and repetition.

This is not just a philosophical or biological point. Because God rules over all rulers, because God calls forth from every human being a unique face of God, each human being must follow God—not Caesar.

If we keep these two passages separate from each other, each seems to be dealing only with a separate aspect of the world. The Talmud is addressing the nature and meaning of human individuality. Human beings certainly are different from each other; is this a cause for contempt, or celebration? Shall we look down on others who are different from us, or honor our very differences as a sign of God's Infinitude? Shall each of us honor in our own selves the uniqueness that makes each of us different from all others—or be ashamed of our own oddity?

And if we look only at the Gospels, this story is clearly political. It begins and ends with a political problem: How shall a devoted Jew, a devoted human being, respond to overweening power in the hands of Caesar?

Put the two passages together, and something happens to them both. When we talk with Jews and Christians about the two passages, their faces change as they fit the two together. They move from curiosity to amazement—even to what the great American rabbi Abraham Joshua Heschel called "radical amazement."

Almost every Christian with whom we have talked about this confluence has said it brings them a new and deeper understanding of Jesus's response—that it seems to be calling for a much more radical refusal to obey the commands of Caesars, much more commitment to follow God.

And almost every Jew with whom we have talked about this confluence has also said it changes the meaning of the Talmud. It gives an activist dimension to the perception of our sacred diversity. It teaches we must not simply bask in the pleasure of our infinite variety, but prepare to affirm it even, or especially, when a Caesar tries to reduce us to uniformity.

And together, the passages also teach us that "giving to God what is God's, to Caesar what is Caesar's" does not demand of us religions that insist on uniformity, religions that pour out the blood of those who walk a different path. That would be to follow Caesar as if Caesar were God, turning Caesar's law of uniformity into a subversion of God's love of differences.

Yet the editors and framers of the Talmud and New Testament took care that both passages appear in neither text. They were walled off against each other. So the second level of wholeness that this reading teaches me is the importance of mending the fringes of the Jewish and Christian traditions.

In Jewish tradition, what makes a garment holy is the careful, conscious tying of *tzitzit*—a certain kind of fringes—on the corners of a piece of clothing. Just as a landholder must let the poor and the landless harvest what grows in the corners of his field, so these corners of a garment remind us that it is not good fences that make good neighbors; good fringes make good neighbors.

What makes a fringe a fringe is that it is a mixture of my own cloth and the universe's air. What makes the sacred Jewish fringes sacred is that they are tied according to a conscious, holy pattern—not left as helter-skelter fringes. They are fringes that celebrate their "fringiness."

That is what we need between traditions and peoples. Not the dissolution of all boundaries, nor the sharpness of a wall, a fence—but conscious, holy fringes.

I think these two passages are among the sacred fringes that define, separate, and connect the two traditions, reaching out as threads of connection that also honor the two different garments on which they are tied.

If we fail to tie such sacred fringes or let them become invisible, the garments lose their holiness.

At first and second glances, the Bible seems to encourage communal identities. It forbids charging interest on loans within the Israelite community, while permitting it toward others. It defines and distinguishes between various cultures that live in Canaan. Even when it talks about the rights of foreigners to work and to eat in the land of Israel, it defines them as different from Israelites. Only rarely does it single out a particular individual within those communities and follow that person with special attention—like Ruth of Moab.

Yet there are ways in which the Bible lights up a laser beam of attention to individuals. The Ten Utterances at Sinai are each directed in the second person singular, aimed at each individual in the crowd that encircles the mountain. Yet the Voice comes from the center, defining the community by addressing every individual in the circle and in effect making each person responsible to all the others when some might break the individual connection.

Indeed, according to the biblical description, when some individuals in the crowd, by worshipping the Golden Calf, violate the covenant even before they have heard its terms, they are punished for their transgression.

Many Jewish prayer services begin with a quotation from a non-Jewish shaman, himself quoted in the Torah (Numbers 24:5). King Balak had hired an expert curse-maker, Balaam, to curse the people of Israel who were swarming across the wilderness after their liberation from slavery under Pharaoh. But Balaam tuned into a spirit-channel that insisted the Israelites, in their commitment to *YyyyHhhhWwwwHhhh*, the Breath of Life, must be blessed rather than cursed.

So as Balaam gazed down upon the Jewish encampment, he proclaimed, "*Mah Tovu Ohalecha Yaakov*—How goodly are your tents, O Jacob!" When the rabbis of Talmud (Baba Batra 60a) read this story, they asked what was so "goodly" about the tents and answered that the doors of the individual tents did not face each other. So no family could see into another family's tent. Each household protected its own privacy and that of all the others.

The ancient rabbis lived under the boot of the Roman Empire, which had a spy system to penetrate any possible bands of troublesome dissidents. So perhaps the rabbis also saw that King Balak was disturbed precisely by this household privacy: How dare these people keep secrets from the king!!

But Balaam saw that privacy was "goodly" and delightful because it was attuned to the uniqueness of each household.

What might this say to us about our privacy not only from the prying eyes of what we officially call our "government" but also from those "private" organizations huge enough to govern much broader aspects of our lives? I mean the corporations that use our own computers to pry into our lives, to turn our every private thought or word or image into money for themselves?

Let us turn with newly open eyes to see what Rabbi Jesus and the rabbis of the Talmud shared as well as where they differed.

For the passages—as connected and as different as they are—teach us that God calls on us to create human cultures that are unique, diverse, precisely because they carry God's Infinite Image—rather than insisting that our cultures, like Caesar's image, be uniform.

Diverse and connected. Judaism and Christianity are unique, and should listen far more closely to each other's wisdoms.

How could we bring these teachings more deeply into our lives?

One liturgical possibility and one in social action.

As congregants of any culture gather in a circle to call each other into community, what if they—we—were to pause to look from face to face around the communal circle, pausing at each face to say to ourselves, "This is the Face of God. And this, so different, is the Face of God. And this, and this . . . Not despite the differences between these faces, but *because* they are so different"? And what if we added the faces of people in New Orleans and Bangladesh, in Tel Aviv and Gaza City, in Tehran and Washington?

And when we examine the use of torture by governments we like or dislike, what if we asked, "Do we become images of Caesar if we torture the Image of God?"

At one level, this story from the Bible and its interpretations by different leaders of the Jewish community living under Caesar's heel may seem to focus simply on the sacred individual, regardless of community. It might seem to justify and support the culture of individualism that characterizes American society.

But it seems that this understanding would ignore one crucial aspect of the story: All this begins in the Image of God. There is Something that connects the different faces of Divinity. It may not be a specific community—Romans, polytheists, Christians, Jews all bear the Image. But each Face, each individual, is rooted in connection, in a Unity beyond the Self. Each human being would not even exist if not for the Creator Who coined the coins and shaped the Image on them.

So if we go deep into each unique separate face, at the root there is the connection that we name God's Image. But each face also faces outward into the uniqueness of each other face. Looking outward, is there only strangeness—or can connection shine there too?

And here I want to share a newer story about this story, a story that rises from and beyond God's earthquake in our lives.

A story that comes, I think not accidentally, from an eight-year-old child—my grandchild. This is the same grandchild who, almost ten years later, declared their self "them" beyond binary in gender.

My wife and I were visiting family in the American Midwest. By sheer accident, the visit came on a Shabbat when the Creation story, including the original tale about the "Image of God," was being read in synagogue.

I said to my oldest grandchild, then eight years old: "Today the Torah says that God created human beings in God's image. What do you think that means?"

Grandchild: "What's an image?

Me: "Ummmm, like a photograph."

Grandchild: Silence. Then, "That's strange. God is invisible. How could there be a photograph of God?"

Silence, except for hearts beating and breath breathing. "Maybe it's more like the other way around. There could be photographs of human beings. Maybe God is in the image of human beings."

Silence. "Only it couldn't be just one human being, it would have to be lots. And we are all different from each other."

Silence. More silence, then Grandchild's face lights up. "Maybe we are different from each other the way the pieces in my jigsaw puzzle are different from each other! Then you would have to fit all the pieces together."

Silence. "Then they would be a community, and a community is more like God."

Ah! So the differences between us are not just to be appreciated, honored, as the diverse refractions of the Infinite. The differences *matter*. We are not only rooted in a Unity, we are intended to flower together into a Unity. And we could not do that unless we were different from each other.

This is an ecological, not a hierarchical, way of thinking about God and Humanity and Earth. In ecological thought, the distinctions between species are crucial—and so is the way they fit together to make one changing whole, an ecosystem.

Is it just individual differences that matter in this profound way? Should we ignore or belittle differences between communities? The Qu'ran does not have an "Image of God" passage aimed at individuals. It does have an explicit affirmation of communal difference, rooted in the Creation of humankind:

> O humankind! We created you from a single [pair] of a male and a female, and made you into nations and tribes, that ye may profoundly understand each other [not that ye may despise each other]. (Qu'ran 49:13, modified Yusuf Ali Translation)

This is ecology translated from biology to culture and society. The differences between us are crucial to make possible a living, flowing unity. This teaches individuality but not individualism. It has strong implications for a politics. It celebrates each version of the Infinite, but recognizes that this honoring of each version only works when we care for each other.

Finally, the question that I raised at the beginning of this chapter: Does it matter today, what sages taught thousands of years ago? I think it does, for three reasons.

First, intrinsically, precisely because these teachings have been taught and retaught, reinterpreted, across centuries and millennia, they bear the imprints of many different times and places. Throwing them out would be like throwing out a family's precious jewels, handed on from generation to generation —Great-Grandmom's wedding ring, Pop's pipe—with all the stories that surround them. Tossing out our treasures of art and music, as if Beethoven became irrelevant once we heard John Coltrane.

Second, because even in an age of distaste for what to many seem the frozen dictates of these ancient stories, there are millions who listen to them and might hear them, unfrozen, in new ways.

Third, precisely because in the midst of earthquake we may feel untethered, despairing, unable to reinterpret how to dance. In this chapter I have woven together different teachings of five sacred texts: the Hebrew Bible, the Gospels, the Talmud, the Qu'ran, the jigsaw puzzle of a twenty-first-century child. The weaving of these threads together is itself a way of dancing in the Earthquake. Communities and traditions that would have been blind and deaf to each other a century ago can see a rainbow of possibilities today.

A rainbow in motion. A rainbow dancing. A kaleidoscope.

8

Toward Justice: Brothers' War and Reconciliation

From almost the beginning to the very end of the Book of Genesis, one theme whirls through many variations: war and peace between many pairs of brothers and one pair of sisters. The pattern teaches us a great deal about not only the politics of families, but the politics of whole societies—not only the politics that is, but also the politics that should be. The politics of God. So let us listen to these tales.

The war between Cain and Abel is the first event outside Eden, the first event of "normal" human history.

Abel, the second-born child whose name means "Puff of Breath," and Cain, the first-born, whose name means "Possessive," bring offerings to God—the fruit of their labor in field and pasture. Abel's offering is accepted, Cain's is rejected.

Cain is angry. What else would you expect? But he says nothing.

God speaks the first word: "Why are you glowering?"

God waits. There is no answer. Instead Cain tries to turn his flaming face away, lest it betray his anger.

God tries again: "Why has your face fallen? If you intend good, lift it up!"

If we think of Cain and Abel as our own children, we might imagine ourselves as parents telling them: "Look at me! Talk to me! Answer me!"

Cain still gives no answer. Hearing none, God continues, "If you do not intend good, sin crouches at the door. Its urge is toward you, but you can rule over it."

Cain gives no answer to God.

Instead he "speaks" to Abel, to his brother.

Kills him.

Wait. Cain *seems* to speak to Abel, but the text is very strange: "Cain said to his brother Abel . . ." What? What did Cain say? In most such passages of Torah, what follows these words is a quotation: a saying. Just above, the same words about God "saying" to Cain are followed by what God said.

But here there are no words, there is no quotation. Some contemporary translations leave an empty space, three dots, a silence. No more can Cain speak to Abel than to God.

So the story continues, wordless, "So it was through their being in the fields that Cain rose up against his brother Abel and killed him."

Again with our own children vividly before our eyes, we could see the story in a new way. We could see them refusing to face our own parental challenge, failing to encounter us—and taking out their anger on each other, on someone weaker than an awesome parent.

But why is the Parent so terrifying? Why did God reject Cain's sacrifice in the first place? And once Cain got angry, would there have been no better, gentler way for God to invite Cain into an encounter? Surely we can share Cain's initial anger at his Parent's favoritism. And even though we are filled with horror at Cain's twisting of his anger against God into violence against Abel, we can still empathize with the fear that made him do that twisting.

Perhaps by this point in the story, God the Parent, Reality, looked grim and awesome. God had told Eve and Adam to choose a life of unknowing blissful childhood, and they have refused. They have chosen instead to grow up, leave childhood, shape their own futures, even at the risk of death.

Their choice of independence hurtles them into a world of scarcity, where food comes hard, through sweaty toil. And nurturing comes hard too: there is a dearth not only of material support, but of love and acceptance. God can respond fully to just one brother.

Which brother? The easy choice would be the older one. The one who in every family already is bigger, stronger, when the younger sib arrives. The one who gives his parents their first assurance of a biological future. The one who in many social systems, including the Israelite law of inheritance, wins more wealth and deference than his younger sibs.

But God responds not to the older Cain but to his younger brother, Abel. In a world of scarcity, God reverses the "natural" order.

Amidst these narrowed choices, God calls Cain to what is a redemptive choice. If you want to grow up, grow up all the way: Face God fully. Argue. Put your anger into words. This encounter is what God invites Cain into.

But Cain rejects adulthood. Perhaps he is afraid. Or perhaps he hears his parents' wistfulness for Eden; so instead of growing up into a new relationship with God, he tries to regress to a still older one. Nostalgically he tries to remain a child. But there is now no bliss in childishness. To be childish now means to be sullen and resentful. To be sullen now means death.

So Cain bequeaths to human history the long, long struggle to grow beyond the sullen rage at life that tricks us into murder of each other.

"Grow up!" says God. Challenge Me, answer Me, wrestle Me. That is adulthood.

If we fail to wrestle God, we will murder a brother; just as it is only when Jacob learns to wrestle God that it becomes possible for him to make friends with his brother.

If we refuse to speak truth to power, says the story, we will end up speaking lies or silence to the powerless—and doing murder. If we refuse to see clearly, truthfully, the world our parents have bequeathed us, says the story, then we will be unable to make the world we want to make.

Neither sullen nor nostalgic, says the story—for sullenness and nostalgia are the degenerate shapes of anger and of love. Better clear anger and clear love, with all their risks.

But the Bible then moves on from the saga of the mothers and fathers of the human race to a smaller arena, the mothers and fathers of the Jewish people.

Here again we hear the motif of the brothers' war, in a series of variations. There is even a story of two sisters' struggle.

And in these stories, something new happens: The conflicts are warlike but not fatal. Indeed, in each generation, the outcome is a reconciliation, until the brothers' war itself can be extinguished—or can rise to a new level.

It is almost as if God learns from the mistakes and failures of the earlier saga of Cain and Abel, and starts over to work things out another way. It is almost as if the writers of the Book of Genesis are calling on us all to learn from the fatal failures of our earlier history and start over to talk things out another way.

So now we enter the saga of the children of Abraham. Generation after generation in the saga, there rises the issue of "first-bornness." It is settled differently from its settlement in the story of Cain and Abel. There God chooses the younger, but the older rejects that settlement. So the conflict becomes irreconcilable, and the first-born "wins": he destroys his younger brother.

In the Abrahamic saga, generation after generation, God again—as with Abel—chooses the later borns. But in this saga, the first-borns "agree" to lose. They lose in power and in blessing, both as a channel of material prosperity and as a channel of redemption. And unlike Possessive Cain, they step aside.

By doing this, by stepping back, they make it possible for the conflicts to be reconciled. Generation after generation, the stories end not with death but with a fragile peace in which the younger brother holds the limelight.

The Bible focuses on Isaac rather than his older brother Ishmael. Yet Ishmael is not left empty; he is blessed as forefather of a people. What is more, the two brothers meet in grief and love when their father dies and choose to live together at the Well of the Living One Who Sees Me.

The Bible focuses on Jacob, whose name in Hebrew means he is the "Grabby Heel" of a guy, who with his mother's and God's help tricks his father into giving him the first-born's inheritance and blessing rather than his older brother Esau. But Esau is not left empty; he survives with many flocks and followers to establish his own people in Edom. Many years later, Jacob and Esau are able to meet lovingly after decades of separation. How do they get there? First, let's look at a closely related story.

In this story, it is two sisters who enter into struggle. Jacob, now living far from his original home, wants to marry Rachel, a younger sister to Leah. But their father is wedded to the "Elders first" rule, and tricks Jacob by secretly arranging for Leah to replace Rachel in the wedding bed. In the morning, when Jacob complains, his new father-in-law even jabs at Jacob's past by telling him, "*Here*, we follow the Elder-first rule!" They arrange for Rachel to become Jacob's second wife.

The struggle between Leah and Rachel starts on that wedding night and continues as they compete over which will bear more sons to Jacob. Over the years, neither sister wins a clear victory in love or child rearing, and neither achieves a full reconciliation. Yet one of them calls this competition an "*Elohim*-

struggle," a God-struggle, in which she is able to "prevail." That very language points back and forward to the Jacob–Esau battle. For it is a foretaste of the later and more famous night when Jacob, frightened of reencountering his brother, wrestles God—and prevails. He chooses to wrestle God—a lot harder and more dangerous than grabbing at his brother. (He walks away with a permanent limp and muscle disease.)

What does it mean to wrestle God? I think it means to say, to scream, "Why is the universe set up in such a way that in order to become who I know I needed to become, I had to lie and steal and cheat my brother and my father?" It means to challenge not his competitor but the system in which they are both caught. It is in that dark night of the soul that the Grabby Heel "Jacob" is renamed "Yisrael," Godwrestler. The next morning, he and his brother can hug and kiss. Challenging the system has dissolved it. His new name he passes on to the whole Jewish people. Godwrestlers, we are called to be.

In the next generation, the Bible focuses on Joseph, second youngest of twelve brothers. He rises above them all and, after a story of fury, hatred, and separation, is reconciled with them. And then, Joseph's two sons test out the final resolution of the issue.

What happens with these two sons, Ephraim and Manasseh? Jacob, their grandfather, insists on blessing them. Jacob, who had fooled his father into giving him the first-born's blessing, leaps across a generation to end the collision over firstbornness. Jacob, who has learned how to stop wrestling with his brother and wrestle with God instead, shows Manasseh and Ephraim how not to wrestle with each other.

Jacob recognizes and affirms his own victory over his first-born brother by reversing the hands with which the blessings should be given. The right hand—the first-born's hand—he reaches out to Ephraim, the second-born. The left hand—the second-born's hand—he reaches out to bless Manasseh, the first-born.

His son Joseph objects: "You got it backwards, Dad!"

Jacob laughs. "Just who are you trying to teach about first-borns? My whole life is about that!"

And in the same moment that he "gets it backward" he dissolves the tension, for he blesses the two boys simultaneously, in the same breath, with a single blessing that they both can hear, saying, "By you"—a singular "you," each of them singularly at the same instant—"shall Israel bless, saying, God make you as Ephraim and as Manasseh."

And indeed Jewish tradition teaches to this day that children be blessed, that they be as Ephraim and as Manasseh. But why these two? Why not as Joseph the ruler over Egypt, or as Jacob who wrestled God, or as Abraham who went on the trackless journey? Because here at last are two brothers who share the same blessing, who do not have to suffer exile or separation or despair or death for each other's sake. Says Jacob, your blessing as a people is to be like these two: blessed in your loving friendship, in your ability to go beyond the brothers' war.

Why all this concern over the war between the first and second brother? Why should it permeate the Book of Genesis? Because with it the Bible accomplishes a marvel of two-level teaching about God's politics. First, it teaches that the first-born is not to dominate—almost certainly a teaching intended to criticize, reverse, and resist a social politics in which the first-born won wealth, power, and blessing simply by virtue of birth. (That was lawful in most of the ancient Middle East, and it was the norm in the Torah's law of inheritance, even though these stories that negate it describe themselves as earlier than the law of first-born privilege.) Second, the Bible teaches that the second-born is not supposed to rule either. What is supposed to happen is reconciliation and finally the dissolution of the conflict itself. But even the dissolution of the conflict must keep its memory alive, or else the tugs of blood, fondness, charisma, and power may revive, and people may regress to letting the first-born rule again.

What a subtle teaching of how to end domination!

To a modern hearing, the brothers' war seems real enough—ask almost any brother, almost any sister. And this struggle among age mates still burns. Ask the schoolchildren of Columbine, Colorado. But even this seems not the sharpest struggle of our public lives. Perhaps the substitution of women for the second-borns in these stories and men for the first-borns would carry something like the same trumpet blast of liberation. Try it: the women who have for centuries been powerless "win," time after time—but each time there is a reconciliation. As the prophet Leonard Cohen put it in his darkly patriotic song "Democracy Is Coming to the USA," singing in the midst of furious feminist demands for justice and freedom, "It's coming from the women and the men. O baby, we'll be making love again. We'll be going down so deep the river's going to weep, and the mountain's going to shout Amen!"

Indeed, we might read this saga of the powerless younger brother who comes to the fore as a tale about not only brothers but also other pairs of powerless and powerful: the poor facing the rich, immigrants facing the home-born, Blacks facing Whites, women facing men, Jews facing Gentiles, the gay facing the straight, the beyond-binary-gendered facing everybody else, the crippled facing the able-bodied, the speechless trees and ozone facing the talkative human race. All the disempowered of our own society, in their relation with the powerful.

Read this way, the saga loses none of its power for talking about the uses of power in that smallest of societies, the family. It loses none of its energy for laying bare the agonies of those who literally are brothers, sisters—still, today, at war and struggling to make peace. But the saga gains power and energy if we hear it speak to every collision of the powerful and powerless in which we act and live.

It gains power and energy for change if we can identify ourselves with Isaac, Jacob, Joseph struggling to win, free of the power their older brothers are born to—and then can identify ourselves with Ishmael, Esau, Judah struggling to win free of the humiliation and the weakness their younger brothers have put upon them. So just as Cain's murder of Abel is the first consequence of exile from Eden, the teaching of Ephraim and Manasseh is to be the key to reopen Eden. It is the Cain and Abel story that must be overcome if the gates to reenter Eden are to open.

So the threads of Genesis lead us to this new beginning, beyond the brothers' war. The new people acting on its new knowledge is to be one model of how the human race as a whole might redeem the world.

One model. The model that can end in reconciliation. Yet we move from Genesis into the Book of Exodus, and there it looks as if the model vanishes. In Exodus, God calls Israel God's own "first-born." This is patently untrue, since Israel is the newest and poorest of the peoples. Egypt and Babylon are far older, richer, more powerful, smarter. So God once more reverses the "natural" order, and chooses as first-born a pack of slaves.

But now the story changes: Egypt, the Older Brother, refuses to step back as had Ishmael, Esau, Judah. Like Cain, Egypt insists on its older-brother status, by insisting on keeping the Israelites as slaves. But this time a God who has grown in experience through the generations of Abraham will not permit the older, stronger, to keep enslaving the younger, weaker brother. So in Exodus, liberation cannot be achieved until the powerful have been shattered and the oppressed have departed, once and for all. With Pharaoh there seems to be no reconciliation. (In the Qu'ran, Pharaoh repents at the last possible moment.)

We will in a moment explore more deeply this other version of God's politics, the pattern inscribed in Exodus. But let us note now the Exodus has impressed itself with far greater power than has the brothers' peacemaking, upon the minds of every people that has learned the Torah or such secularized analogues as Marxism. Exodus became the model for modern revolutions, national and social, where the saving remnant hoped to wipe out oppression and corruption, depart physically or politically from the oppressors and corruptors, and remake their country. The pattern has been so powerful that we have paid little attention to the alternative that emerges from Genesis: the war and peace of brothers.

Yet the Prophets of Israel looked beyond the Book of Genesis to see a future in which, "In that day, Israel shall be the third alongside Egypt and Assyria, each a blessing in the midst of the earth—for YHWH of the multitudes has blessed each, saying: 'Blessed be Egypt My people, and Assyria the work of My hands, and Israel My inheritance'" (Isaiah 19:24).

The model of the brothers reconciled.

Today we face many struggles where we do not want to destroy the oppressor or separate into a new society. Instead we need liberation with reconciliation. Not the gruesome grin of the powerless commanded to love their taskmasters, nor the gracious smile of the powerful who are glad to love their serfs. But the free laughter of wrestlers, where the grapple of liberation and the clasp of love are intertwined.

How many of us, women or men, want women to be freed from men by smashing men and leaving them? How many of us, Black or White, want Blacks to be freed by smashing America or leaving it? How many of us want Earth to win its freedom from human ravishment by destroying Homo sapiens?

Exodus may be the last resort in every struggle. If we must, we must. If the stronger refuse to step aside, then like Pharaoh they may end on the ocean floor. Or the weaker, like Abel, may end up dead and bloody in the open field. But as the Prophets taught, the story does not end there, must not end there. Neither ocean floor nor blood-soaked field is the gate to Eden.

9

The Sin of Economic Injustice; The Blessing of a Pulsating Economy

Keep the Sabbath day by hallowing it as YHWH your God has commanded you. For six days you are to serve and to do all your work; but the seventh day is Sabbath for YHWH your God. You are not to do any work—not you nor your son nor your daughter nor your servant nor your maid nor your ox nor your donkey nor any of your animals nor your sojourner that is in your gates—in order that your servant and your maid may rest as one like yourself. You shalt bear in mind that serf were you in the land of Egypt, but YHWH God took you out from there by a strong hand and by an arm outstretched to sow seed; therefore YHWH your God commands you to keep the day of Sabbath-ceasing.

—Deuteronomy 5:12–15

> *At the end of seven years, you shall make a Shmita—a Release. This is the point of the Release: Every possessor of a loan of his hand shall release what he has lent to his neighbor He is not to oppress his neighbor or his kinfolk, for the Release of YHWH has been proclaimed!*
>
> —Deuteronomy 15:1–6

Moving from the collisions and reconciliations of individualism and communalism, we see the Bible addressing two questions at their sharpest and their deepest:

> What do the rich owe the poor, the community, and God?
>
> What does the whole community owe the future as a sacred economic process and intention?

The national origin story of the Jewish people, their governing legend, was (and is) that they began as a band of runaway slaves who in their flight sought to create a new kind of society. In that society, the memory of going forth from slavery, and the constant Presence of a God Who had made it happen, would always tug toward social justice and against the privileges of wealth and power.

The annual lifting of that memory when a million people would gather in Jerusalem to celebrate the overthrow of a tyrant kept the urge to freedom alive. That was the energy that infused the "Palm Sunday" march led by Rabbi Jesus, against the Roman Empire and its local puppet government.

That March began just a few days before Passover. After all, if you were a Jewish activist who intended to challenge an Empire, what could be a better time of year than one that recalled the fall of Pharaoh?

There followed a nonviolent assault led by Rabbi Jesus on those who profited from the Imperial economy through money-changing at the Temple. Then came a few days of agitation in a city full of restless Passover pilgrims and a Passover Seder of the inner council of the Movement. The Seder was infiltrated by a paid undercover government agent, for the Empire could hear the whisper of a danger that was growing toward a growl.

That well-tuned Imperial ear led to the arrest of Jesus, his death by torture under the direction of Rome's procurator, and the arousal of a transnational movement remembering his extraordinary life and death. And Life.

That movement, which became what we know as Christianity, emerged alongside a new kind of Judaism. This new path of Jewish religious life centered on words of prayer and reinterpretation of words of Torah rather than on Temple offerings.

For the new Jewish community, Passover remained central in a form that more and more supplanted the Temple pilgrimage: even before Rome destroyed the Temple. That form was the Seder, reminding people to remember liberation through words and questions, rather than the lamb offered at the Temple. The words were still accompanied with foods: the bitter herb of slavery and the unleavened bread of the poor, transformed by urgent action into the bread of liberation.

For the other emerging Jewish community, rooted in memories of the charismatic rabbi from the Galilee, what became central were the Holy Week that grew out of Jesus's attempt to repeat the first Passover by dissolving a tyrannical Empire, and a ceremony of shared bread and wine that grew out of Jesus's leadership of the Seder.

Alongside Passover, and connected to it, were two living practices that shaped the economic vision and reality of the people.

They were the experience for centuries of a lived weekly Shabbat and a lived Sabbatical Year. They built in a profound institutional leaning against privilege.

At the head of this chapter is the passage from Deuteronomy that sets out the meaning of Shabbat: on every seventh day, there is to be a universal Sabbath-pausing from all work. Through the power of this pause, every Israelite and every foreigner and immigrant takes on an equal dignity, whether rich or poor, a landholder or a landless orphan, a woman or a man. And even the animals, wild or domesticated, get to rest.

This overarching value is, according to Deuteronomy, the central symbol of Israel's covenant with God. It is directly connected with the Revelation at Mount Sinai.

This universal pause is explicitly connected with the liberation of the people Israel from slavery to Pharaoh in Narrowdom (as we might translate *Mitzrayyim*, "Narrowness," the Hebrew name for Egypt). Slaves are not allowed to rest; all who can claim a time to rest are free. Not slaves.

It is especially important to notice that this version of the Fourth Commandment differs from the version in Exodus. In Exodus, the reason given for Shabbat is that it is a memorial of the cosmic pause that caps the story of Creation. Here it is said to be about ecosocial justice and equality.

Deuteronomy claims to be Moses's memory and storytelling of what had happened in the Wilderness. Modern scholars are convinced that the Hebrew of Deuteronomy comes from a period later than Exodus—around the time of Jeremiah, when there were strong social divisions within the Kingdom of Judah, and strong demands for justice.

It is reasonable to imagine that a prophetic voice that arose in those days decided to demand radical social change by amending the text that commanded Shabbat, so that it would speak for social justice more than for cosmic rhythm. That same prophetic voice may well have felt that the outcry would gain more strength if it were directly connected with Moses himself as its author. The Prophet Huldah, who discovered a Scroll that was probably Deuteronomy hidden in the recesses of the Temple, may even have written the Scroll she claimed to find.

Deuteronomy also goes beyond the earlier Leviticus text we have discussed in Chapter 1 about the seventh year, the year when the land and the people get to rest. Deuteronomy decrees that in that year, all debts must be released, remitted, annulled, forgiven. The Leviticus text goes out of its way to assert that this teaching comes, like the teaching of the weekly Shabbat, on Mount Sinai. So in both these ways Deuteronomy demands a profound amendment to the Revelation at Sinai.

This release from debt becomes so crucial in daily life that the word for "release"—Shmita—becomes the name traditionally given the seventh year. In rabbinic tradition, we hear it even more than the title *Shabbat Shabbaton*—Sabbath/Pause raised to its own exponential value—that it is given in the Leviticus passage demanding that the Land be allowed to rest.

Why are these Deuteronomic Amendments to the Israelite Constitution so important, even beyond their specific content? Because they strengthen our understanding that Torah emerges not only from the agreed assumptions of Israelite society but also from struggles against those assumptions—including the struggle for social justice, against oppressions by the rich and powerful.

The struggle against official assumptions about "stability" still stirs us. The Shmita/Sabbatical Year created an economy utterly different from what Rome then and Modernity now assume is valuable. Rome and Imperial Modernity celebrate unending "economic growth." *The biblical intention was not unending growth but pulsation—a time of gentle growth followed by a year of pause, inwardness, and sharing.*

In Israelite memory, Egypt had been a place where economic, political, and religious power was all held in a single person: Pharaoh. There was a memory, possibly shared with the Egyptians, of a time when yeoman farmers owned their land. But in the memory of the runaway slaves who became the people Israel (or in a cautionary tale, an elaborate parable), in the midst of a terrible famine, the yeomen had become sharecroppers. They sold their land to Pharaoh, in extortionary exchange for food from previous harvests so as to get through the famine with their lives. Their goal was unchecked economic increase. Only a famine could interrupt it, and the result would be a concentration of economic power.

So for the new society in Canaan, defining itself as the runaway slaves who had fled an Egypt that enslaved them and enserfed the ethnic Egyptians, the question became, do we want a society of unchecked acquisition, enormous economic inequality, and concentrated economic power? Or do we want one that undergirds a constant return to near-equality among all residents? We know that constant economic effort for MORE becomes not just an effort but an unending economic race: some become wealthy, others are reduced to poverty.

Should we instead try to create an economy that lives a rhythm of growth and restful pause, growth and restful pause—a pulsating economy, not one committed to unceasing growth? An economy that never gets far from economic equality?

They chose the second future.

The Shmita was probably the most encompassing approach to shaping a future of equality. But there were smaller policies and commitments that moved in that direction. Let us look first at the Bible's effort to encourage a measure of economic equality. It may be one of the most widely known aspects of the Hebrew Bible—perhaps equally with the oft-repeated command to "Love your neighbor as yourself," and "Love the stranger, for you were strangers in *Mitzrayyim*" ("Narrowdom," the name of Egypt in Hebrew).

Indeed, the reference to being "strangers" in Egypt and therefore subject to economic exploitation may hint at an economic inclusiveness in the new land.

(The word "*Mitzrayyim*" actually means "Land of Tight-and-Narrow." In the Bible's teaching of geography and history, that "Narrowdom" was the name of what we call Egypt. Perhaps it was evoked by realizing Egypt was a long narrow strip of farmers living close to the Nile River. For Israelites, perhaps the name triggered memories of the Narrow Place of their enslavement.)

This social imperative is so woven into the fabric of the Hebrew Bible (and thence into Christian and Muslim teaching as well) that there is no one pithy line of text to sum it up.

Look at this array of varied texts. They all see extreme economic inequality as troublesome. They begin by looking only at the home-born citizens of the people Israel and then expand their vision. Perhaps they realized that equality only within the community would be weakened if neighbors were unequal. So they propose several different ways to deal with it.

- *Deuteronomy 23:20–21:* "You are not to charge interest to your kinfolk—interest in silver, interest in food, interest in anything for which you might charge interest. To a foreigner you may charge interest; but to your kinfolk you shall not charge interest, in order that YHWH your God may bless you in all that you put your hand to, in the land where you go in to possess it."
- *Deuteronomy 24:14–15:* "You are not to withhold from a hired worker who is poor and needy, whether he is one of your kinfolk or one of the sojourners who are in your land within your gates. On his payday you shall give him his wages, before the sun sets (for he

is poor and for it lifts his life-breath), lest he cry out against you to YHWH [the Interbreathing Spirit of the world], and there be sin upon you."

- *Leviticus 19:9–10:* "When you reap the harvest of your land, do not reap to the very edges of your field or gather the gleanings of your harvest. Do not go over your vineyard a second time or pick up the grapes that have fallen. Leave them for the poor and the foreigner. I am YHWH [the Interbreathing-Spirit of all life]—your God."
- *Deuteronomy 23:15–16:* "You are not to hand over serfs [indentured servants] to their masters those who have sought refuge with you from their masters. Let them dwell beside you, among you, in the place that they choose, wherever in your gates [your boundaries] seems good to them. You are not to maltreat them!"

These passages set forth distinct responses to economic inequality. The one on "gleaning" requires that as a matter of absolute right that applies throughout society, the poor—home-born or foreigners—must have access to a "paying job" very like the kind of work that most members of the community are doing. The pay is in food that the gleaner works for. No land-holder may turn away a poor person from his field. Others speak to specific cases.

When must a wealthier person pay a worker that he has hired to do specific work? The answer is before the sun goes down. When indentured servants or slaves have fled from their master, should they be sent back? No, they must be allowed to settle wherever they choose "within your gates." This seems to apply to either an Israelite or a foreigner whom we might call a refugee seeking asylum.

At some point, the society, or some voices within it that we would now call prophetic, seems to realize that legal provisions are not enough. Maybe people were ignoring them, or side-stepping them. Maybe passion felt lacking—passion to uphold the law or even go beyond it. So we get the following.

- *Isaiah 58:6–8:*
  This is the kind of fast that I desire:
  Unlock the hand-cuffs put on by wicked power!
  Untie the ropes of the yoke!
  Let the oppressed go free,
  And break off every yoke!

  Share your bread with the hungry.
  Bring the poor, the outcasts, to your house.
  When you see them naked, clothe them;
  They are your flesh and blood;
  Don't hide yourself from them!
- *Amos 6:1–7:* "Woe to those who are at ease in Zion—Those who lie on couches of ivory and loll on their beds, who feast on lambs of the flock and calves out of the stall; who hum snatches of song to the tune of the lute; who drink from basins of wine, and anoint themselves with the choicest oils, and feel no pain concerning the destruction of Joseph.

  "Therefore, they shall be the very first to go into exile—yes, become refugees!—and no longer shall they dine at haughty banquets."
- *Ezekiel 18:10–13:* "Suppose he has a violent son, who sheds blood or does any of these other things (though the father has done none of them):
  He eats at the mountain shrines.
  He defiles his neighbor's wife.
  He oppresses the poor and needy.
  He commits robbery.
  He does not return what he took in pledge.
  He looks to the idols.

> He does detestable things.
> He lends at interest and takes a profit.
> Will such a man live? He will not! Because he has done all these detestable things, he is to be put to death; his blood will be on his own head."

The ancient rabbis thought the Prophet Isaiah's outcry (58:6–8) important enough to designate it the Prophetic reading for Yom Kippur. It calls not for individual charity but for society-wide commitment to help the poor. It speaks also to what we would call "mass incarceration" ("the handcuffs put on by wicked power") and connects it with poverty.

Amos bitterly attacks the uncaring rich. There is no comparable biblical passage that attacks the poor as lazy, immoral, or improvident. Indeed, the pattern in our own society is exactly the reverse: Adulate the rich, scorn the poor.

All of these diverse approaches to a just economics make even stronger sense if we take into account an underlying truth about the people Israel: Not only do the land and the people rest, but the normal social system itself rests. Not only are debts annulled but even the fences between one landholder's property and the next are torn down, so that people and animals can freely wander, sharing the unfettered, unsown, unharvested abundance freely given by the Earth.

By the standards of Modernity, this whole way of living is not just a sin, it is anathema. The Industrial Revolution, the Computer Revolution, on our way already into the Robot Revolution powered by Artificial Intelligence—faster and faster, no Shabbat, no Shmita to pause and reconsider. The next technology, and next, and next, seem so attractive and so powerful, so beneficial.

So seductive is this race for techno-wealth that it is hard to pay attention to its downsides. The multiplication of Homo sapiens drives other species to extinction—including those on whom the human race depends. The multiplication of CO_2 and methane drives the planet into furnace heat, and we suffer wildfires, supertyphoons, hyperdroughts, and monsoons. Yet Modernity is geared to prevent any pause, any Shabbat, any Shmita, to reconsider. We are taught to fear what we might lose if we paused to reevaluate.

But if we were to set aside one year in every seven to rest and reconsider, that would require not rejecting all technology but reflecting, choosing with awareness. There is a profound connection between the pulsating economy and the rhythmic reaffirmation of ecosocial justice.

When the moderately rich could not multiply and magnify their wealth by lending money, charging interest, keeping the capital to multiply forever, they could not become Hyperwealthy. When the richest landholder had to pause even from sowing seed and pruning grapevines and harvesting barley for one year out of seven, there was a rhythmic decline in his wealth so that he, too, might share without accumulating. And as they paused from multiplying their wealth, it became harder and harder for them to keep dominating political life, religious life, cultural life.

What would such a pulsating economy mean in our own day? Let us take into account two major differences between the biblical Shmita and our own society.

First, the Bible was written out of the experience of one small people who lived in one small sliver of land. In our era, almost all human beings live in a tightly woven fabric that intertwines all communities and all species on the planet. Even if the poorest people on the planet never get to see the internet or ride an elevator to the hundredth floor, we are all bound together now by the plastics in our oceans, the chemicals in our air.

Second, for the ancients, the sacred relationship between Earth and human earthlings was far more often embodied through food than by any other means. Food was brought as offerings to God. There was a sacred code of practice around food, called *kashrut.*

The sabbatical pause of Shmita was defined chiefly around what food could be raised, when. Today, our relationship with the Earth depends as much on the consumption of energy as on the eating of food.

What does this require of us? Is there a way to re-create a pulsating economy based on rhythmic pauses in the harvesting of energy and the accumulation of money, as the Bible did by pausing in the harvesting of food and by rhythmically annulling debts? Would making sure the Earth completely rests from two centuries of overdosing it with carbon dioxide and methane, while carrying out a sweeping installation of solar and wind energy, be one way of moving into a pulsating global economy?

Imagine announcing a six-year plan of federal grants to make sure that every building in the US secures its electricity from wind or solar power, preferably through a neighborhood co-op. Would one way of nurturing a pulsating economy be to require that in every seventh year, every large corporation would have to convince a regular civil jury whether they should be able to renew their corporate charter or had failed in their duties to customers, workers, neighbors, and the Earth—and must have their charter to do business lapse? Would strong government encouragement and support for neighborhood-based co-ops drawing on wind or solar energy help us move into a pulsating economy?

Imagine that personal debts up to, say, $70,000 were annulled every seventh year in exchange for investing the next six years in public service as teachers, nurses, road builders, renewable energy engineers and installers, trash collectors, tax collectors, and other vital tasks.

Imagine a minimax wage law providing that the maximum yearly income for any worker in any enterprise can be no more than seven times the income paid to the lowest-paid worker.

Imagine that one year in seven, all the technologists and engineers get paid to take a year off, on condition they will spend the time not reinventing but reconsidering. Talking with each other, with poets and painters and pianists, with prostitutes and priests and politicians, with thirteen-year-olds and eighty-three-year-olds, about the meaning and the impact of technology. Imagine that when they come back to work, they are free for two more years to develop the technologies that they, not their bosses, want to make happen. A kind of nonacademic freedom for engineers.

Imagine making federal grants to neighborhood organizations to create their own folk festivals for a full week, twice a year, when "normal business" comes to a halt and only the work of emergency life-saving continues. The same week everywhere in America, to celebrate *E pluribus unum*—our unity born of diversity. To fill us with the joy of knowing that everywhere among us, in all our differences, we are acting together.

Imagine creating publicly owned banks that invited deposits from the local public and were committed to lend money to local enterprises and needy persons. No doubt it will take an uphill struggle to make those who benefit most from "economic growth" accept living instead in a pulsating economy. What would make victory in such a struggle possible?

We might be moved to act if opinion leaders, especially leaders of religious and spiritual communities, insisted that the public consciously face that there will be a wave of death around the planet if we do not make this transformation. But fear alone will not convince us. We must fill not only the goal but the process with joy and celebration. A solar co-op must be not only a money-saving, a neighborhood-healing, even a planet-restoring enterprise, but also a community of song and home cookery and storytelling.

These suggestions are simply ways of putting hypothetical flesh on the hypothetical bones of a pulsating economy. We need such flesh to make the dry bones live. But it will take the strong devoted Breath, the Spirit, of many active people to breathe life into the possibility.

10

Warlike Kings: A Blessing or a Sin?

"These will be the ways of the king who will reign over you: He will take your sons and make them serve with his chariots and horses, and they will run in front of his chariots. Some he will assign to be commanders of thousands and commanders of fifties, and others to plow his ground and reap his harvest, and still others to make weapons of war and equipment for his chariots. He will take your daughters to be perfumers and cooks and bakers. He will take the best of your fields and vineyards and olive groves and give them to his attendants. He will take a tenth of your grain and of your vintage and give it to his officials and attendants. Your male and female servants and the best of your cattle and donkeys he will take for his own use. He will take a tenth of your flocks, and you yourselves will become his slaves. When that day comes, you will cry out because of the king you have chosen for your-

> *selves, but YHWH/Yahhhh/the Breath of Life will not answer you in that day."*
>
> *But the people refused to listen to Samuel. "No!" they said. "There must be a king over us. Then we will be like all the other nations, with a king to lead us and to go out before us and fight our battles."*
>
> —1 Samuel 8:11–20

The biblical vision of political and religious leadership—centralization or decentral authority, a king or no king, violence or nonviolence, constant war or universal peace—is profoundly ambivalent. At one point the people demand a king because they need a warlike leader; but the danger of a warlike king is what worried them most. How to deal with the dilemma?

From looking at the Bible's attempt to create a pulsating economy, we must turn to look at what for many societies is the least pulsating institution—the official government. Indeed, many modern scholars define a "government" or the state as that institution that possesses a monopoly on the legitimate use of violence. Monopolies are the opposite of "pulsation."

For centuries, the Bible says, the people Israel lived with a governmental arrangement far from a "monopoly" of violence or of religion. The people was a loose federation of tribes in which sacrificial offerings were carried out in many places, in which emergencies were addressed by charismatic leaders called *shoftim*, "judges." They came to the fore when they were needed to defend the poor of Israel against oppressors or to defend the people as a whole against another community. They were much more like charismatic leaders than like the presumably neutral, top-down "judges" that today sit in black robes on elevated benches.

And then the Bible describes a struggle: Is this loose confederation far too weak? Some foreign nations come equipped with a powerful king who can unite their nation to attack Israel. Should the people Israel have a king, like all the other nations, in order to defend themselves? Or to attack?

The argument is crystallized in a three-way debate among the people, the Prophet Samuel, and God.

The people tell Samuel they need a king. Samuel and God first point out that Israel already has a King: the one in Heaven. For them to seek a king is equivalent to their constant desire, ever since the Breath of Life has lifted them out of slavery, to worship idols. When the people answer that they need an earthly king, Samuel and God warn that he will conscript their young men for his army and his young women to serve as cooks and attendants in his palace. The people shrug off these warnings, too.

So God (remember, one way to think of God is as the Holy Process by which consequences flow from our decisions) shrugs, too, and tells Samuel to choose a king for them. Samuel chooses Saul, a king who veers between mania and depression—perhaps suffering from what we would call bipolar disease. Perhaps Samuel deliberately chooses the people's first king to be troubled and troublesome, lest the people become imprinted on the notion that kingship is a wonderful solution to their woes.

Once there are kings, there must also be prophets. The role arises by which the Breath of Life can, through a prophetic voice, come as both the warm breeze of everflowing love and the disappointed hot, hot wind. Breathing the words of the Interbreathing Truth, the prophet can confront the king and point to the vision of a Beloved Community.

But experience convinces Torah writers by the time of Deuteronomy that prophetic outbursts are not enough. The new

Scroll, in what we may see as an extremely distant ancestor of the US Declaration of Independence, puts explicit limits on the powers of an Israelite king. Among them, twice repeated, are limits on his war making powers: He is not to multiply the horses he would need for aggressive imperial warfare. He is not to pay the extremely high prices necessary to buy them, for that would require imposing extortionary taxes on the people, forcing them to return to the Tight and Narrow Space equivalent to slavery in Egypt (Deuteronomy 17:1–20).

The king must not pile up money for himself as a side benefit for his service to the people. He is not to multiply wives for himself, lest the sexual overload distract him from the public good. And he must sit before the priests who are part of the tribe of Levi, to read aloud from Torah these passages that limit his power and other passages that protect the poor.

This last provision is fascinating. You might say that assigning oversight to the priests was an attempt to do then what we attempt to do now with the Supreme Court. The biblical provision for priestly review may even seem slightly more realistic than our Supreme Court review. For the biblical priests and the king had separate power bases. (The priests were rooted in the tribe of Levi, and the royal line descended from David of the tribe of Judah.) The Torah "Constitution" may have thought that the priests could not be overawed. But there is no suggestion of how their supervision of the king's recitation can become more than literally listening. Can they, do they, interrupt in public to say, "That last line you read about not equipping your army with chariots—Have you obeyed it?"

Our Supreme Court seems less independent from the get-go, because it is appointed by the president whose authority it judges. Does it defer to presidential power? Up to some limit, our experience shows that the Court draws on public confidence and its life-long terms of office to strike down presidential actions that go beyond the rules. But our experience also shows that beyond some "normal" limit, the more egregious the president is in breaking rules and limits on presidential power, the more likely he will be able to shape or overawe a Court so that it defers to him.

The biblical system of priestly review totally broke down after the Maccabean rebellion. The priestly Maccabees led a guerrilla war against the foreign occupation by a Hellenistic Syrian emperor, who had Hellenizing allies among the Jewish people. But when they won what became a civil war, their heirs quickly used the power they had gathered to grasp the kingship and combine the powers of the Temple and the throne. This was an unconstitutional usurpation, and led to a corrupt deal with Rome. But the people had little recourse. The double question the Bible raised three thousand years ago remains alive today: Is a constitutional limited monarchy necessary to uphold the poor and the nation's independence? Can a limited monarchy be kept within its limits?

The Torah prescribes one more biblical attempt to reinforce the dialogue between King and people. The same Book of Deuteronomy that struggles toward social justice reports in the name of a Moses who is very close to the end of his life:

> At the end of each seven years, at a fixed time on the festival of Sukkot, after the year of release, when all Israel comes to present themselves before *YHWH* [Breath of life] your God, in the place that He will choose, you must read this Torah before all Israel, so that they will be able to hear it. "You must gather together the people—men, women, children, little ones, and resident-sojourners—from your settlements, and let them hear it. They will thus learn to be in awe of *YHWH* your God, carefully keeping all the words of

> this Torah. Their children, who do not know, will listen and learn to be in awe of *YHWH* your God, as long as you live in the land which you are crossing the Jordan to occupy." (Deuteronomy 31:10–13)

This immense gathering is called "*Hak'heyl*," meaning "Assemble!" Is it intended to be only a top-down teaching, in which the people are merely listeners? It is hard for me to believe that such an assemblage would not be also an invitation to the people to make known their own demands for justice according to their own lights.

Remember, this same moment at the end of the Shmita year is when all debts were to be annulled. Perhaps at this assemblage was the moment when the people could make sure that debts were in fact annulled, that wages were indeed being paid by nightfall. When the people assembled, were they the only listeners, or did the king and other official leaders also need to listen?

So we see several ways in which the biblical teachings attempted to awaken the rudiments of popular power as checks upon the king. Yet we can see that the Bible reaches toward solutions but does not achieve them. It honors limits on the king but cannot enforce them. It affirms nonviolent resistance to tyrannical acts but cannot invent effective forms of nonviolent power. It celebrates the Prophets' call for transnational and international peace but cannot deliver the institutions that could achieve it.

The Bible casts even more doubt on the ultimate value of war by setting rules to govern the gathering of an army. Torah provided for individual exemptions from the army:

> Then the officers shall speak to the people, saying, "What man is there who has built a new house and has not dedicated it? Let him go and return to his

> house, lest he die in the battle and another man dedicate it. And also what man is there who has planted a vineyard and has not eaten of it? Let him go and return to his house, lest he die in the battle and another man eat of it. And what man is there who is betrothed to a woman and has not married her? Let him go and return to his house, lest he die in the battle and another man marry her." (Deuteronomy 20:5–7)

The age of military service was from twenty to fifty. Let us note that these men who are exempted are likely to be exactly the young men in their early twenties whom most armies in the world today try hard to conscript or persuade into military service.

And then an extraordinary leap:

> "The officers shall speak further to the people and say, What man is there who is fearful or soft-hearted? Let him go and return to his house, lest the heart of his brothers melt like his heart." (Deuteronomy 20:8–9)

Rabbinic commentators say that the man who is "fearful" is afraid to be killed. The one who is "soft-hearted" is unwilling to kill.

No one needs to persuade a draft board that he fits these categories. If he claims them, that's it.

This seems to me an astonishing way, on the one hand, to make sure that the people's army that actually goes into battle is stalwart, so deeply committed to the values at stake as to be willing to kill or to die. And it also recognizes something akin to what we might call conscientious objection. What's more, if a large number of men of military age feel the case for war does not meet their standards, the army might well be far undermanned, and the war may be impossible.

The Maccabees (1 Maccabees 3:55–56) actually applied these rules, even in the extreme case of a war to resist an occupying army that had desecrated the Temple and was forcing people to worship idols.

And finally, even if there is war—

> When you besiege a town for many days, waging war against it, to seize it, you are not to bring ruin on its trees, by swinging an axe against them, for from them you eat; you are not to cut them down—for are the trees of the field human beings, to come against you in a siege? Only those trees of which you know they are not trees for eating, them you may bring-to-ruin and cut-down, that you may build siege-works against the town that is making war against you, till its downfall. (Deuteronomy 20:19–20)

So the Torah views war as likely, even on some occasions as necessary; but it sets limits to the system of conscription and limits to the kind of war the community can fight. We will come back to these limits to see how they might lift up some guidance to us today.

Now let us move past the rules of "ordinary" warfare to early events in the development of what we call "nonviolent resistance" and "civil disobedience."

We have already seen how the Exodus story gives us two women who were perhaps the first in human literature to nonviolently resist a governmental decree. They were the two midwives who refused to obey Pharaoh's order to kill all newborn Israelite boys. The text is deliberately muddled over whether the resisting midwives were Israelites, or Egyptians, or a two-person international feminist conspiracy reaching across national boundaries. And their refusal was followed by an act even more recalcitrant and explicitly transnational:

Pharaoh's own daughter not only pulled the baby Moses out of the water but then acted with the help of Moses's sister Miriam to nurture the foundling child whom she is supposed to drown.

She names him, too, perhaps prophetically seeing that he will challenge the entire Egyptian social system. For in the Egyptian language that she knew, "Ra'meses" was "Son of [the sun-god] Ra," and "Thutmose" is "Son of [the god] Thoth." The name "Moses" would mean "Son of______" with an empty space for the father of this foundling: As a foundling, he is "Son of Whoever." Or as the coming leader of a movement that would overturn all the well-known, well-named gods of Egypt, he is "Son of the Unnameable." Son of the One Whose Name is just a Breath. Or—perhaps the child whose father is unknown is precisely the child whose father is the One. A startling affirmation of profound resistance to a domineering social system!

The process of liberation in the Exodus itself is woven with violence in the form of disastrous ecological upheavals and ultimately the death of Egypt's firstborn. But the imposition of these plagues is ascribed to God as a consequence of Pharaoh's cruelty—and thus placed one giant step away from Israelite behavior.

Indeed, the Israelites are specifically forbidden to leave their homes on the night when all the firstborns of Egypt die. Why? To prevent the "messenger" [or "angel"] of "death" from entering upon them, or even within them. Some have interpreted this to mean they must stay in their own houses lest the impulse to kill enter within them.

The next morning, when they leave their homes to begin the Exodus, they leave through a doorway whose margins they have smeared with blood. The only bloody "house" through which all humans leave our homes is the womb. In the moment before Exodus, the entire people is reborn, like one newborn nonviolent baby.

Then the most active deed of the Israelites themselves is described as a nonviolent one: visiting the Egyptian homes to demand reparations—gold and jewels that will repay them for many years of slavery. (The Bible requires that when an Israelite indentured servant leaves servitude in the beginning of the seventh year, there must be a severance payment to account for years of unpaid work.)

So the Exodus is itself the first great story of mass nonviolent resistance—a general strike. And there are others. The Hebrew Bible describes nonviolent resistance to Babylonian and Persian power.

For example, Jeremiah warns against using violence and military alliances to oppose the Babylonian Conquest, and argues instead that God will protect the people if the Kingdom of Judah acts in accord with the ethical demands of Torah—the proactive nonviolence of freeing their slaves and letting the land rest. The community hearkens as Babylon besieges Jerusalem. When they free their slaves, the Babylonians retreat as Jeremiah had prophesied. But the people, relieved of their fears, take their slaves back again—and Jeremiah tells them they have by their own act of violence forfeited God's protection. The Babylonian army returns, and this time sacks the city and burns the Temple.

This story lifts a deeper question than its factual recital: Were the Babylonian withdrawal and return supernatural miracles, or did the prophet discern a truth of human action and military strategy that boastful kings and slave-holders ignored? Once the slaves were freed, the Babylonians might have faced a city unified, in which everyone was prepared to resist an empire that would enslave them all. Best for the empire to pull back. When former slaves were robbed of their brief liberation, class conflict might well have weakened the will of the city to resist. The imperial army saw its opportunity renewed, its conquest eased.

The deeper teaching? That to be a "prophet" means to hear the deeper truths of history, to know how societies behave when their rulers are too drunk with power to know the perils at their feet. To hear the subterranean trickles of the Truth that acts have consequences—not to hear the commands of a King on high. The prophet not only hears the deeper truth—but also speaks it out despite the threats that speaking brings from those in power. Even speaking can become a form of nonviolent civil disobedience.

Daniel and his friends famously are cast into the lion's den for nonviolently refusing to obey the king's command to worship foreign gods.

And, although the Book of Esther ends in Jewish "counterviolence" that goes beyond self-defense, Esther herself demonstrates nonviolent civil disobedience when, in fear and trembling, she approaches the Persian king without having been invited so that she can carry out her mission to save the Jewish people from a murderous tyrant.

Well, we might say, it is not surprising that Israelite culture would celebrate resistance to foreign potentates. What about Israel's own kings?

Here too there are tales of nonviolent resistance. There is a powerful story of an Israelite king, Saul, who had to deal with an underground guerilla whom he thought of as a terrorist, named David. David, with a very small band of underground guerillas, went off, hungry and desperate, and found food and protection at a sacred shrine in the town of Nov. There they asked the priests to let them eat the showbread, the *lechem panim*, the sacred bread placed before God, because they were desperately hungry. And the priests fed them from the sacred bread.

When Saul heard about this, he said (more or less), "Anybody who harbors a terrorist is a terrorist!" (do you hear an echo?), and so King Saul ordered his own bodyguards to kill the priests of Nov. But the bodyguards refused.

His own bodyguards, yet they refused to murder these priests! An act of nonviolent civil disobedience against an Israelite king, not an Egyptian Pharaoh!

The tales of the prophets are filled with moments of nonviolent resistance to illegitimate uses of power by Israelite kings. Jeremiah, for example, used acts of street theater to protest. (Think of the "Yippie" actions like throwing dollar bills onto the floor of the New York Stock Exchange and making a spectacle of the ensuing wild scramble to gather them—street theater against the greed of these "pillars of society.")

Jeremiah wore a wooden yoke as he walked in public, to embody the yoke of God that the king had shrugged off and the yoke of military defeat and Babylonian Captivity that the king was bringing on the people. When someone else, claiming the mantle of prophecy, broke off the yoke from Jeremiah's neck and proclaimed that all was well and the people were in no danger, Jeremiah went home to meditate and get in touch with his whisper of Divinity, his hearing of the Breathing winds of change, his deepest understanding of his own people and of the threatening empire. He came back wearing an iron yoke.

And of course we know the prophetic teachings that lift up the vision of a world at peace, when nations will "study war no more" (Isaiah 2:4), when the sacred Menorah itself will light up the wisdom of "Not by might and not by power but by My Spirit, says the Infinite Breath of Life" (Zechariah 4:6). What then might we draw from this examination of the biblical wisdom about violence and nonviolence?

For me, the answer is clear. We now have available to us a great variety of means to act nonviolently to hobble and deflect a government's intent to mount an illegitimate war or to attack its own community. Yet wars and even genocides continue. What has failed?

The hope that requiring legislatures to decide whether to make war, rather than leave the decision to notoriously mercurial kings, has not prevented immoral and illegal wars. Neither has forbidding war by treaty, even when the treaties create elaborate institutions like the UN. Why have solemn treaties, elections, and meritocratic appointments by those elected failed to prevent war?

Let us look at, and beyond, the Bible's stories of nonviolent resistance to violence by those in power. In our day, if we adopted training in the philosophy and practice of nonviolence as necessary to civic competence, as we claim to do with learning to take part in elections, could nonviolent resistance to violence become more successful?

In some of the most successful uses of civil resistance, it has flowered from deep roots of a spiritual element. It almost always requires spiritual depth to assert that one's political opponent, even a deeply noxious one, still partakes of a sacredness so profound as to prevent the use of violence. And it often requires spiritual depth to expose one's self during civil disobedience as vulnerable to nasty words, economic reprisal, angry violence, prison, torture, death.

How do we enrich and strengthen this way of carrying out nonviolent opposition to violence? One way of doing this—drawing on God's music to dance in God's earthquake—would be to free the great religious festivals from rote recitation and turn them into authentic carriers into public space of the values they originally asserted.

For example, Passover and the Christian Holy Week that historically and spiritually emerged from it celebrate liberation from a Pharaoh (and later a Roman Empire) that oppressed human beings and brought plagues upon the Earth. Both festivals look toward the creation of new communities of love and justice and of joyful self-restraint in consumption that makes possible healing for the Earth and for the human heart.

Imagine sharing the Matzah and Bitter Herb of Passover as part of a sit-down at the White House. Imagine marching through Wall Street and into the New York Stock Exchange while chanting the same psalm that the Palm Sunday demonstrators chanted as they walked with Jesus from the Mount of Olives into Jerusalem.

Imagine reconfiguring the Stations of the Cross at places of poverty, despair, and violence in a metropolis today, and clogging the streets, stopping all traffic, with bodies of protest at those Stations. (The first part of this, mostly without arrests, has already been happening.)

Imagine—this is much harder—barring the doors of H-Bomb factories or Big Oil refineries while carrying giant crosses and the Torah Scroll, forcing these lethal operations to shut down or to demand that the police desecrate those sacred symbols in order to restore business as usual—the busyness of death.

Imagine observing Lent and the special kosher code of Passover food and the Ramadan total daytime fast from food and water by fasting from Carbon-based energy. By fasting from food grown on the backs of slave labor. By sharing food with the poor, as ways to protect the Earth and its most vulnerable communities.

Further examples include the following: All three of the Abrahamic traditions call for restraints on eating particular foods or on eating at all during particular times (e.g., kashrut and some fast days among Jews, Lent among Christians, halal and Ramadan among Muslims). The Muslim festival of Eid al-Idha celebrates (by sharing food with the poor) the moment when God turned Abraham away from sacrificing his child and instead encouraged him to offer up a ram. Imagine making explicit the hidden meaning of the day under the slogan, "Don't kill children; feed the poor!

And let us pursue the question that these food taboos raise that go beyond what we have known as "food." In our generation, what is "food"? During the long era of human history in which the strongest relationship between human beings and the Earth was through food, these traditions encoded food-oriented relationships with the Earth into a sacred pattern.

In our era, extracting energy from the Earth—from coal, oil, uranium, natural gas, and fracked unnatural gas—has joined the growing of food from the Earth as an equally crucial aspect of the Earth–Human relationship. So this relationship should be encoded into a sacred "eco-kosher," "eco-halal" pattern. To heal the Earth's climate and feed all Earth's people, changes in patterns of consuming food and energy will be crucial.

How do we connect traditional religious practices about food with justice in feeding people and in shaping new sacred practices about energy? Both Judaism and Islam forbid eating pork, and Hinduism forbids eating beef. Could religious communities forbid the use of fracked unnatural gas? Could they all, like Hinduism, declare all beef off-limits because raising multitudes of cattle releases multitudes of methane into our air, helping make the Breath of Life into a global furnace? Could they require sharing a certain proportion of the food a family eats to be given to the poor?

These are, once again, suggestions, provocations toward the new dance steps that we can play with as our dance floor tumbles and twirls. They need to be new but echo the past enough to invite into the dance those who remember a waltz, a square dance, a rumba enough to join the rhythm. If we are seeking to prevent genocides and wars, minimize fire and fury, then we need to multiply the open gateways to new dances of resistance.

For me, the point is that the Bible points the way without arriving at an ever-moving destination. It calls on us to make these visions real. It calls on us to turn its own moments of wistful wishes into sturdy new practices, commands, and commitments.

Tyrannies, wars, genocides, ecocides—like the subjugation of women and all the other tyrannies we have discussed, tyrannies the Bible tolerated and sometimes commanded, even against its own best visions, must become forbidden acts. When they occur, there must already be in place

- Transnational bodies with the will and nonviolent power to mobilize against such tyrannical acts. Transnational bodies of co-op members, of labor unions, of multireligious communities, of women, of students, of various professional associations that mobilize their buying and boycotting power, their sit-down power, their strike power, their power of concerted prayer and pilgrimage.
- International institutions that, unlike the UN and the EU, have elected parliaments with real power to prevent wars, genocides, and planetary ecocide. If elections for such bodes don't exist or the elected bodies have no power, then organize "unofficial" elections like the Mississippi Freedom Democratic Party more than fifty years ago, and send the elected paraofficials to intervene in official bureaucratic corridors.

And above all, the Bible in all its forms, like most of the other spiritual wisdoms, calls forth communities to make these visions real. Rabbi Abraham Joshua Heschel, a devout and prayerful and activist Jew, wrote that

> Prayer is meaningless unless it is subversive, unless it seeks to overthrow and to ruin the pyramids of cal-

lousness, hatred, opportunism, falsehood. The liturgical movement must become a revolutionary movement, seeking to overthrow the forces that continue to destroy the promise, the hope, and the vision.

Ameyn, amen, amin. May it be so, may we make it so.

11

Two Biblical Genocides: Were Both Sins?

It may seem a deep disappointment to descend from images of institutions for a world at peace to listen to tales of genocide—the worst behavior of kings, the most monstrous extension of war.

But in our world, genocides—not only the most famous, the Nazi genocide of Jews—have been too explosive, too much an element of the earthquake we are living through, for us to ignore what we may need to learn from the Bible's teachings.

The Torah tells the tales of two leaders who attempted to commit genocide. One of them failed. One succeeded. The story of the one who failed is famous: it is the story of Pharaoh and the Exodus. The other one is rarely discussed: it is the story of Moses and his leading the genocide of the Midianites (his relatives by marriage). What do these stories mean for us today?

Let us start with the most famous biblical story of attempted genocide and the first story of nonviolent resistance, the story of Pharaoh and what became the Exodus.

But before we enter the story itself, let me step back for a moment to talk with you about how the story sounds when we read it in the world we live in. To me it sounds amazingly familiar as I look at our own earth-quaking world today. It feels as if I could be reading in the pages of the *New York Times* today about Pharaoh and the women who first resist his violence and then the growing movement of Resistance. No, not "could be reading." *I am* reading that story when I open up the daily paper.

Am I just twisting the ancient story out of shape in order to see it that way? I don't think so. But you, my partners in our dance on the Quaking dance floor of our world, will have to judge. Reading the story in the midst of "God's Earthquake" startled me. It may startle you as well.

In many nations, authoritarian leaders and political parties have greatly increased in power, sometimes taking over the government.

Like Pharaoh in the ancient story, they have built a political base from people who feel themselves "forgotten," fearful that the economic and cultural future will leave them and their children out. These authoritarian leaders have turned those fears into fear and hatred of marginal communities—marginal by race, religion, sex, or ethnicity. But in actual policy the leaders have sided not with "the forgotten" who support them but with the rich and powerful, even with those whose wealth depends on destructive exploitation of the Earth itself. Thus, they have brought dangerous "plagues" on their own peoples.

Reread the biblical stories. The similarity between Then and Now is actually remarkable. There are at least three ways of understanding this coherence between Then and Now:

- I could be twisting the ancient biblical stories to fit into my modern understanding of the earthquake where we live.

- OR The ancient story is simply a report of what happened when power ran amok, and the process looks a lot alike whenever power runs amok.
- OR Some brilliant poet/novelist/prophet took fragments of history and wrote a nation-transforming, world-transforming story—the best archetypal tale of power run amok and of resistance that there is. So powerful a tale, so deeply felt in our cultures today, that any leaders in any generation who start to feel the urge to make their power absolute take steps that echo the archetypal story, even unwittingly. And similarly, the story shapes the ground beneath the steps of those who resist such leaders, even if the leaders and the resisters don't glance down to see the ground they're walking on.

Given that modern historians and archeologists see no evidence that the factual history happened the way the story teaches, that last possibility may be the one we come to trust the most. We may feel that the story holds much more "truth" than the facts, just as the fictional play "Hamlet, Prince of Denmark" bears a fuller, deeper truth than the dry and dusty factual chronicles of the Danish royal family.

So let us turn to the ancient story. To understand the Pharaoh who bestrides the beginning of the Book of Exodus, we must go back to the end of Genesis. A previous Pharaoh has centralized all power in himself, following the advice of a clever Israelite (Joseph, whose name means "Increase").

All over Egypt, free yeoman farmers have been reduced to sharecroppers on the Pharaoh's land. They and their families have been forced to move from the lands of their ancestral clans to distant places; so their emotional, spiritual, and political connections, as well as their economic base, have been disrupted. Yet Joseph's family has had a protected allotment of land and privileges in their own district, in recognition of Joseph's service to the crown.

It is easy to imagine (this is "midrashic history," not asserted in the biblical text or in the Egyptian archives) that insurgent energy begins to bubble up among the Egyptians. Grandparent tales of a freer, more abundant, and culturally more resonant life may have started roiling the royal power. And perhaps there was also growing resentment aimed at the protected minority of outsiders who had settled in the Goshen region and were doing well. Even their religion and its practices were alien.

In this quite likely stew of political and cultural trouble, a new Pharaoh comes to power. He has no sense of obligation to Joseph's family, and he needs to deflect the increasing hostility against his own authority.

Ahh! Best to respond not by restoring the local and decentralized yeomanry but by aiming their anger against the Israelites. These foreigners breed far too prolifically; their numbers are a threat. It is easy to stigmatize them as *ivrim*, a word of contempt for people who cross boundaries, the equivalent of "wetbacks" or "rootless cosmopolites" or "globalists" in the parlance of today. (The word "*ivrim*" became "Hebrews" in Western languages.)

Egypt was already a great power, an empire. It had perhaps the strongest army in the region, focused on horse-drawn chariots that small tribal politicians could not afford. But empires never rest easy. They are always concerned about encroachments from other Imperial centers or defiance from small cantankerous communities.

And in the unfolding royal tale of defining the *Ivrim* as a foreign force, it made sense for the Pharaoh to warn the Egyptian public that the Ivrim might side with Egypt's foreign enemies, perhaps become terrorists attacking the old-stock Egyptians whose language and religion they didn't share.

So they must be put under tight control by the state, made to work for the royal family as builders of the warehouses for storing the national food supply, kept in line by overseers who doubled as police. And all of this could be carried out only by making them pariahs in the national culture, separating them from Egyptian share-cropping farmers.

In the old Egyptian culture, Pharaoh was already seen as a god. Now his political and economic power grew even greater. His power went to his head. It began to infect his own outlook on the world. He began to believe his own propaganda about the dangerous Israelites, the Ivrim. He decided they needed to be erased as a separate community. He issued the order to murder newborn boy babies of the Ivrim.

Here you might think bad will become still worse. But the first cracks appear in Pharaoh's authority. Two midwives—and then his own daughter—disobey his decree, as we have already seen. Moses is born, and lives to grow up.

At this point, astonishingly, the story seems to say (mostly through silence) that for eighty years—forty before an adult Moses fled Egypt after killing a racist policeman, forty more while he dwelt in Midian before his experience with the Burning Bush—for eighty years, an uneasy high-tension status quo continued in Egypt. Pharaoh did not pursue his genocidal threat to its conclusion, and the Israelites did not rise up in visible rebellion. Perhaps women continued to pursue their underground resistance.

Then Moses reappears, possessed of a burning new vision, announcing that the very Name of God had changed. Everyone must understand the world in a new way, and then change the world to embody the new vision. The Israelites must be free to leave their forced labor, to withdraw from Egypt, and to explore how as a free people they can serve their new sense of God, create a new kind of society that would fulfill the vision.

And here we see a remarkable unfolding of pharaonic psychology. Moses begins with a seemingly innocuous request: three days of Time Off to focus on religious practices to connect with God. Pharaoh responds not with any effort at accommodation but with more draconic rules of forced labor. The shaken Israelites dissolve completely.

But Moses and Aaron (and, we may imagine, their prophetic sister Miriam) do not dissolve. They challenge Pharaoh more directly and powerfully: the drinking waters of Egypt become undrinkable.

A word about that plague and the ones that follow: One way of understanding them is that God is a Super-Pharaoh in Heaven, like a king imposing more and more dire punishments on Pharaoh and his nation. Another way of understanding is that the deep processes of the Breath of Life, the Interbreathing Spirit of the world, bring about consequences for one's choices. If you sow wheat, you reap wheat. If you sow poison ivy, you reap poison ivy.

That's not a reward or a punishment. It is a consequence. From that perspective, Pharaoh's domineering behavior toward people brings about consequences in the natural world. Sow subjugation, reap a disordered and chaotic Earth—bloody water, overrunning frogs, mad cow disease, unprecedented hailstorms.

In this regard, it makes a difference whether we think of God as King (*Melech* in Hebrew) or Breath/Wind/Spirit (*Ruach* in Hebrew). Now we know, scientifically, what our forebears knew, agriculturally. Farmers and shepherds knew that humans, other animals, and plants were part of an interwoven life that made food possible. (Remember the verse in the second Creation story in Genesis that said human beings needed to emerge before plants, because humans were necessary to nourish vegetation.)

For the Bible, the Name *YHWH* binds all breathing life together. We, the heirs of modern science, know with more precision that we humans, we animals, need to breathe in the oxygen that the trees and grasses breathe out. They need to breathe in the CO_2 that we breathe out. The Breath of Life, *YHWH*, is Echad—One.

The reason Pharaoh was first frightened by each plague and then dismissive was that he thought each one was an accident: "Stuff happens." Moses, Aaron, and Miriam knew that God's new name, "*YHWH*," meant that all life was interwoven and that each plague was no accident. It was a consequence of Pharaoh's own behavior. It was a part of nature, neither unnatural nor supernatural nor accidental. Shepherds and farmers must have known that their own specific work went this way: "What you sow is what you reap." What made "*YHWH*" so powerful was that it extended this knowledge to all life. To politics, to money, to work, to prayer.

Right here we were invited to learn the wisdom that we later encoded in a chant:

> *Sh'sh'sh'ma Yisrael, YHWH/Yahhhh Elohenu, Yahhhh echad.* Hush'sh'sh and listen, you Godwrestlers: The Breath of Life is our God; the Breath of Life is ONE.

One more learning from the plagues: The Torah text starts out saying that after each plague, Pharaoh hardens his own heart. But midway through the plagues, God hardens Pharaoh's heart. If we think of *YHWH* as a King, a Super-Pharaoh in the sky, this seems both unfair and unnatural. But what if we think of *YHWH* as the process that interweaves, interbreathes, all life? Then we can understand the story this way.

Pharaoh's hard-heartedness is like addiction. Take heroin once, twice, maybe ten times, you are still free, making your own decisions. But at some point the heroin takes over. You are not taking heroin; the heroin is taking you. "God"—that is, the interconnections that make for consequence—takes over.

Pharaoh became addicted to his own domineering power. He couldn't stop. Even when his own advisers say to him, "Can't you see you are ruining Egypt, your own country?!" he cannot stop. Even when he is in agony over the death of every firstborn in every Egyptian family, including his own—even when he insists the Israelites leave—in the morning he cannot stand the shattering of his power. He orders his chariot army to pursue the runaway slaves.

He cannot help pursuing them even to the dissolution of his power and his life, as it dissolves in the Sea of Reeds—which becomes the Red Sea from the blood his army sheds. The trouble is that though his arrogance, stubbornness, and cruelty destroyed himself, according to the story he deeply damages Egypt. The Torah goes out of its way to assert that death comes to even the first-born of the slave girl who does the hardest work in Egypt, pushing the great millstones to grind the wheat. She surely had no guilty role in Pharaoh's egomaniacal addiction, but she suffered from his actions. Because we are all affected by the sins of the powerful, we are all responsible to do what we can to prevent them.

So now that you have been reminded of what the ancient story says, does it sound as familiar as the daily news? Do you think I have twisted the story out of shape? I hope that like me you have come to see the story, whether it has nuggets of fact or not, as a brilliant archetypal parable—teaching us, warning us, inspiring us across every generation.

Yet there are surely differences in the way I see the stories from the way they have been taught for at least two thousand years. The most important difference is that all those years "*YHWH*" has been described as Lord, King, Judge, sitting above and domineering over the lives of humanity and all the life-forms of the Earth, beyond what is "natural," impervious to human will.

If instead we see "*YHWH*" as the Interbreathing through which humanity creates natural consequences for itself and all of life, then human choices, human actions matter. The ultimate Pharaoh brings on his own society the ultimate earthquake.

And the biblical history—whether history or fiction or parable—brings this archetypal wisdom to every generation. Including our own! It is living through this earthquake today that stirs me, us, to this new way of seeing. For now the earthquake is powered by new technologies that human beings have brought into the world. We are in fact not merely clay shaped by the hand of a great inscrutable Potter. We ourselves are both the Potter and the Clay. Our new-found power is so great that we stand on the verge of poisoning the clay, shattering the pots and the potter's wheel.

Let us take up the Torah's second case of genocide—this one not only successful, but seemingly approved by God and Moses (Numbers 25:1–9, 14–16).

The story begins when Midianite women and Israelite men defy the laws forbidding a sexual relationship between them. As a result of their relationship, a plague breaks out among the people.

This may not be a supernatural tale of an angry, punitive God. When two cultural communities meet that have had no previous contact with each other, there is often an outbreak of communicable diseases that had by "natural selection" been tamed in each community but become intensely virulent when the other community comes in contact with it—especially sexual contact. For example, Europeans suffered a lethal version of syphilis and the Native communities of Turtle Island suffered a lethal version of measles after the European invasion of what became known as the Americas.

In the Torah story, however, *YHWH*, the Breath of Life, whispers into Moses's ear a tale blaming the disaster on the

Midianites. What was their guilt? Midianite women, say God and then Moses, seduced Israelite men into sexual relationships and into foreign forms of worship.

We should pause to note that Midianites were the community into which Moses had married after he fled Egypt. Was he himself "seduced" by Tzipporah? His own father-in-law was a priestly leader of the Midianites, whose experience and wisdom had guided Moses in his leadership of the Israelites. Did he convince Moses to introduce "foreign forms of worship" into Israelite practice?

Is the story hinting that a leader of wisdom and adeptness can be trusted to oversee and absorb contact with a different religious community, but an untutored public cannot?

The result had been a plague. Moses understood the Breath of Life, the Wind of Change, to be taking on the attributes of Hurricane. Protecting the people Israel by destroying the people of Midian, Moses heard himself commanded to lead the Israelites in "taking vengeance" on Midian for their women's sexual and spiritual attractiveness.

Why does Moses accept this command of "vengeance," and even define it expansively as genocide? Just because the whisper comes from a Voice he has learned to trust? If that "still small voice" comes within him, why is that the Voice his innards generate?

Is it because Moses, whom Torah calls the humblest leader of his era, believes that whereas he can cope with "intermarriage" and intercultural intertwinings, the people as a body cannot? Is it because *YHWH* tells him that after this vengeance against his own adoptive people, Moses will "be gathered to his people"—that is, will die with them? Is he consumed with a sense of failure, and so falls into depression, despair, and cruelty?

So Moses decrees the death of every male Midianite and every woman old enough to have been sexually active. And the Israelite army had sufficient military power and sufficient willingness to "follow orders" that they carried out his command.

It is clear that the Torah responds differently to genocides directed against "us" (e.g., by Pharaoh) and to genocides carried out by "us."

But very few of us read this story with equanimity or pleasure. What are we to do with this story? How can we treat as sacred text a tale that fills us with sorrow, disgust, horror, indignation?

Even if this genocide actually happened, why did our religious leaders down the centuries affirm that it should remain—including its aura of Divine and Prophetic approval—in the sacred text? Why could it not have been reported along with condemnation? "A radical failing," the text might have said. "Moses misunderstood God, and for this terrible mistake was barred from entering the Promised Land." Good questions. No answers—not at first.

In 2016, we read this story in the regular schedule of Torah readings during the same week in which the Movement for Black Lives, an outgrowth of the Black Lives Matter movement, published a Platform that dealt with many issues of racial injustice.

One small plank of the Platform accused the modern State of Israel of a genocidal policy toward the Palestinian people. Even worse, there was no condemnation of any other nation that was behaving in ways similar to Israel—for example, China in Tibet. It was one thing, some of us thought, for Jews or Palestinians or other Arabs or Muslims to single out the Israeli–Palestinian conflict for unique attention. But why would African Americans be doing that? Was there an overtone of anti-Semitism in this condemnation?

There was an intense eruption of fury from many organizations in the American Jewish community. Some even announced they would no longer cooperate with the Black Lives Matter movement on any other issues, even clear cases of racist oppression in America.

Watching some Jewish organizations refuse to work with any aspect of Black Lives Matter, I noticed that the same organizations had not taken the same approach to the Roman Catholic Church. Even though the Church had used its power for stands about gay rights, abortion, and birth control that to most Jews were horrendous, the same organizations continued to work with the Church on issues like immigration where both communities shared the same values.

Why this difference? Why did seeing alliances as complicated —not all-on or all-off—make sense when it came to the Catholic Church but not when it came to Black Lives Matter?

Because Black Lives Matter was, well, Black?

Because it had far less power than the Church? (Indeed, it had far less power to hurt Israel through one sentence in a paper Platform than the Church had to damage gays and women, including Jewish gays and women, through its huge lobbying wealth and numbers. That might have made these Jewish groups more wary of the Church than of Black Lives Matter. But no.)

Because the third-rail issue to these Jewish organizations was Israel, while the rights of women and of GLBTQ communities were far less important?

Meanwhile, some Jewish organizations announced that they thought the accusation of genocide was a serious and hurtful factual mistake, that they would dialogue with Black Lives Matter to reexamine the facts and hope to come to a different conclusion, and that they would continue to work together when there was clear agreement on the issues.

I thought Black Lives Matter was wrong. I had long recognized that the government of Israel was oppressing Palestinians, but I did not think the oppression added up to genocide. On the other hand, some researchers argued that the word had been used by some genocide scholars to mean oppressive measures that pointed in the direction of mass death, even if there was no formal decision to bring about mass death, as there was with the Nazis. In the African American community, it was suggested, the word had for some taken on that looser meaning.

And I certainly did not intend to abandon or ignore the entire Black Lives Matter movement, which had made visible some of the worst but unseen aspects of American racism. Nor even to write off just the Platform, which I thought was, except for the single sentence, an extraordinarily accurate and creative assessment of the changes we need to make.

So, despite my upset at what I thought a false and hurtful comment, and taking into account the complexities of politics and language I had seen, I joined with those Jews who thought it was important to "connect and criticize" to enhance the relationship through honest dialogue.

And beyond that, I was struck by the coincidence of reading the Torah passage on the Midianite genocide and the accusation against the modern State of Israel in the same week. What struck me? I realized that some of the Jewish anger at the Black Lives Platform came from a sense in the Jewish community that Jews could never commit genocide, and everybody knew that. So the Platform was especially outrageous.

But I had just reread the story of the genocide of Midian. We *could* do that, the Torah said. We *did* do that, the Torah said. With God's permission, at God's command.

Was there some possible value, after all, that we could glean from this disgusting Torah story?

What came to me was that we could learn precisely from our own disgust and horror. We could treat the Torah passage as a warning. A warning that "we"—whatever "we" you like—

are not immune to the genocidal impulse. The "we" might be the Jewish people facing Palestine, or the American people facing Natives, Blacks, Latinos, or Muslims; or the Buddhists of Myanmar facing the Rohingya Muslims; or the rulers of Saudi Arabia facing the Shia community in Yemen.

Always within each society is the potential of defining some weaker community as so thoroughly "outsiders" as to make genocide possible. This impulse we must guard against, and in our generation we can take the passage on the Midianites as precisely a reminder to ourselves to stay on guard against it. If some "we" is accused of genocide, we must take the accusation seriously and examine ourselves.

Then we can correct our behavior or refute the accusation. Or both. For such an accusation from a usually responsible source is likely to mean that some of our own behavior points in that direction and must be corrected.

Even in the story of the genocide of Midian and even more in the commands of Torah about the laws of war and of kingship, there are some hints of ambivalence about war.

One unexpected aspect of the Midianite genocide might inform our attitudes and behaviors toward "ordinary" wars, pogroms, and lynchings even if they are far short of genocide. After telling the Israelites to kill every male and every adult female, taking the young girls as booty, Moses instructed them, "Pitch camp outside the communal camp, for seven days; everyone who killed a person or everyone who touched a corpse, decontaminate yourselves on the third day and on the seventh day, you and your captives" (Numbers 31:19). Only after twice immersing themselves in water along with their weapons, clothing, canteens, and their booty could the men of war return to the broader community.

There was here perhaps a rudimentary sense that after obeying a bloody command, even one that came from God and the prophet-in-chief, one might be imbued with posttraumatic stress, carrying blood in heart and mind, and would need a process, a practice, to release one's self from the obsessive focus on killing or being killed, raping or being raped. This at least we might hear as a shred of wisdom amid the stink of genocide. Today we might apply it to all the "victors" and victims of such violence.

Is genocide a sin? Of course, despite what the Bible seems to say. But telling the story of a genocide is a sacred obligation, on one condition: that we learn from the story that no nation, no government, is immune to the temptation, and that we must learn the story in order to prevent it, not to imitate it.

Coda to the Dance

Eden Once Again?

Several years ago, I spoke at the Chautauqua Institution on "What Is Radicalism?"

I began by pointing out that the Latin root of the word "radical" means "root." Radicalism means going to the root, and for me the Bible is the root of my thinking and could be one root of a decent society, a Loving and Beloved Community.

To bring some humor into what might easily become a tense conversation, I explained that I was dressed in a red shirt and white pants because these were the colors of a radish. Again, the root of "radish" means "root." A radish and a radical have much in common.

My talk was about the transformation of biblical religion that the Bible itself requires—demanding that we, the human race, grow up into a true adulthood. Many of those ideas are what I have deepened in this book.

Then there was a question period. One of the audience members challenged me: If I were so rooted in the Bible, what did I make of the line, "Be fruitful and multiply, fill up the Earth and subdue it?"

There was a buzz, a mutter of approval in the audience. Caught the rabbi out, eh?

I waited till the buzz died out, till people were ready once again to pay attention.

Then I said, "*Done!*"

For a moment people caught their breath, making sure they had heard right, just a single word. Then there was a roar of applause.

I waited till the applause died down, and then I added, "*What now?*"

In the era of human history that the Hebrew Bible grew out of and addressed, the world human population was about twenty million. It was easy to imagine and to hope that our numbers could greatly grow, even if the Israelite community and many others were attuned to a pulsating economy.

Now our numbers are approaching eight billion.

We may have already reached the level at which the planet can bear no more humans, certainly not if we insist on walking into the future our present Modern high-tech, high-income, economic "growth" life path. Because of our numbers and our technology, we have initiated the Sixth Great Extinction in Earth's history. We have invented nuclear weapons that could destroy all life, and we have emitted CO_2 and methane that are wrecking the web of life that has existed since Homo sapiens evolved. We have indeed "filled up" the Earth and "subdued" it.

The whole era of Torah that was signaled by those words has ended. What was a joyful blessing has become a sin.

What now?

Time and thought that move always in a straight line are liable to march off a cliff. Time and thought that move always in a circle are liable to get stuck, to die in the repetition of old formulas in new realities.

The spiral gives life. Reach back to old wisdom to make new truth. Create a rhythm in time that reminds us to work and reflect, work and catch your breath, work and make music, work and dance, work and make love. When you take up the work again, there will be some new flavor in it.

Let us hark back to that story of the Garden where we began, where the journey of us all began. And hear it anew.

The story of Eden is a tale of children growing into rebellious adolescence and then into an adulthood of drudgery and hierarchy. The Bible asks us, God asks us, Reality asks us, can we grow up some more?

Can there be a Garden for grown-ups? Can we learn from the mistakes we have made? Can we then dance our way into a Garden that notices our earlier missteps and heals them?

The Song of Songs welcomes us into that grown-up Garden, and beckons us to becoming a fully grown-up human race.

What does it mean to be more fully grown up?

In Eden, Papa–Mama God commands us. In the Song of Songs, the specific *YHWH* Name of God nowhere appears. For those who opposed the inclusion of the Song in Holy Writ, this absence of the Name was a sufficient reason. But Akiba thought this absence was most holy. Why?

Like grown-ups, in the Song we have absorbed the wisest teachings of our parents and have grown an ethic of our own. Our Mama–Papa God does not need to be present, visible. This is a sacred stage in the maturing of our species.

What is the ethic that as grown-ups we have made our own?

The ethic of love. Love is strong as death, says the Song. In the Song's vision of a future reality, sin is not utterly banished from the world. After all, the Beloved's brothers beat her up when she goes out at night. But the world has been profoundly transformed. In the world as we know it, distrust and violence are pervasive, and love gleams like fireflies in the darkness. In the world of the Song, love is pervasive, and sinful violence has been dissolved into small smudges.

What love is so manifest in the Song?

No longer are the Earth and human earthlings at war with one another. The humans are not grasping, not gobbling the Earth. We eat joyfully of fruit and nuts, wine and spices. We do not kill even a carrot, a radish, by ripping it from the Earth. The Song becomes the menu for the holy day of Tu B'Shvat, Yahhh B'Shvat, the Full Moon fifteenth day of the midwinter lunar month of Shvat. In that midwinter moment comes a festival of trees reborn, The Tree of Life Reborn. And the Song becomes the recipe—fruit, nuts, spices, wine—for the inmost secret sacred food we eat for Passover—*charoset*, the Holy of Holies on the Seder plate. The vision of a world in loving does not require killing.

And just as we do not kill and do not gobble up the Earth's abundance, the Earth is generous to us. Our mother does not wound us with thorns and thistles but nourishes us in green and fruitful joy.

The ethic of love. The Song shows us a sexuality that is free and bold and joyful as it would be for fully mature adults—not shameful as it came to be in adolescent Eden, not forced upon subordinates as we learned would be our lot as Eden crashed. Sexuality in the Song is not severed from the Spirit but united with It. In the Song as a vision of the future, we do not have to choose—as the ancient Rabbis did—between seeing the Song as an allegory of love between God and Humankind, or as a celebration of erotic love between human beings. The Song begs us to hear the Song as both, and One.

The ethic of love. Hierarchy within the community is almost gone. Surely in the content of the Song: The shepherd and his lover meet, depart, reunite. There is a chorus of the women of Jerusalem, a recitation by the man and woman of the beauty of each other's bodies, a celebration of the beauties of the Earth.

The ethic of love. Not only in the content but also in the form, modern scholars of poetry argue: Is it a coherent single poem, or a collection of poems brought together?

Why do the scholars argue? If it were a single poem, surely there would be a plot, a story? At first it seems there is. But then the story vanishes. And just when the reader is convinced there are a series of unconnected poems, the story returns. And vanishes. Even though the Song is so erotic, there is no climax, no orgasm. All loving foreplay. Even at the end, the lover vanishes somewhere in the mountain ranges of the North.

The ethic of love. Even in the sense of time that the Song provides, fluidity is what we hear. "Do not rouse love, or lovers, till they please." A refrain that comes and goes. A spirituality of time not organized by clock and calendar as is the Talmud of the male rabbis ("From what time till what time may we recite the evening prayers?" begins the Talmud).

The ethic of love. The Song sings out a grown-up world where women have come into their own, where men are also free, not subjugated. A world where it would even be possible to imagine and celebrate gender beyond the binary.

Eden for grown-ups. The problem with eating from the Tree, it seems, was not only the danger of gobbling up the Earth and all abundance. The parable gives a certain character, a meaning to the forbidden Tree. And here too, we humans are beginning to grow up.

The story seems to point to two Trees. One Tree whose fruit is good and evil, up and down, mine and yours, this and that. Every this and every that. The other Tree grows in the flow of life, and gives forth the flow of life. No "this," no "that."

Yet some mystics have taught that the most profound mistake was thinking that there were two separate trees. Thinking that it was even possible to eat from the Tree of Distinction and not from the Tree of Flow, or vice versa. We must learn, these sages taught, that there was always and forever just one Tree. Then we could live again in Eden.

How could this be? How could Distinction and Flow not be always two different kinds of fruit the world has set before us, saying "Choose!"

Here is how: Think of the world that ecology describes. In that world, it is crucial to know how this species differs from that, how with different mouths they feed each other, eat each other. And in that world, it is crucial that all these distinctive beings flow their lives together. Each breathes the other. Precisely because they are distinctive, they are able to make flow.

Hush from braggadocio and listen up, all peoples, each people, every people. Your own unique way of breathing is a necessary part of the universal breath. The breath of many lives is the Breath of Life, and the Breath of Life is ONE.

It seems to me no accident that this fuller understanding of Eden, Song, and God; of work history and women is coming true, and due, at the Turning Time of all of human history.

We grow up in our relationships with each other and the Earth, or we die. The triple tale of Lot's daughter, Tamar, and Ruth make sense together only as they point toward the messianic moment. We are seeing history change as women are empowered; we are seeing history change as traditional notions of sexuality and gender turn fluid; we see history change as we realize that we are neither masters nor stewards nor victims of the Earth, but part of it. Sometimes masters, sometimes stewards, sometimes victims—always part.

Will we grow up enough to make the choice? To abandon the most dangerous and destructive sins of all, the sins of subjugation that will destroy ourselves and Mother Earth and choke to death the Interbreathing Spirit of all life, the *Ruach HaKodesh*?

Will we grow up enough to give birth to that Loving and Beloved Community in which all life-forms can breathe deep?

What now? That. Now.

Forethought in the Form of an Afterword

When you're 86, the task of identifying and thanking your most important teachers feels like jumping into a rushing river. The lesson: It takes more than a village to make a transformation. It takes a river that itself is always changing—a river of people who connect, divide, flow, eddy. And the river itself is made up of many rivulets of different flavors and fall lines and intensities, sparkling brooks and curly creeks, great broad expanses of slowly flowing dignity and muddy fertile deltas. So has been the river I have drunk from, swum in, gazed at.

First, this book itself: I have dedicated it to my closest comrade in thinking, feeling, learning, teaching, writing, taking action, and loving—my rock in the rushing river, Rabbi Phyllis Ocean Berman. And more: herself a transformed and transforming person in her own worlds.

Beneath my urge to think deep into history and the future are the following:

- Some of the best of speculative fiction, including Walter M. Miller Jr.'s *A Canticle for Leibowitz*, Ursula K(roeber) LeGuin's alternative-anthropological novels *The Left Hand of Darkness* and *The Lathe of Heaven*,

Bernard Malamud's *God's Grace*, Marge Piercy's *He She and It*, James Cameron's film *Avatar*, and Richard Power's *The Overstory*;

- Kenneth Boulding's *Conflict and Defense* and *The Meaning of the Twentieth Century*;
- Many historians of Judaism who have explored the great shift from biblical Israel to Rabbinic Judaism and Christianity, under the pressure of Rome and Hellenistic civilization. Among these are Mordecai Kaplan's *Judaism as a Civilization,* which looked at successive versions of Judaism as linked but distinct civilizations deeply affected by the civilizations around them;
- Evan Eisenberg's book *The Ecology of Eden,* which dared to fuse history, anthropology, ecology, and the study of religion into a masterly examination of the earlier great shift under pressure from the Babylonian Empire, from a buzz of Western Semitic cultures into what we know as biblical Israel and the Hebrew Scriptures; and
- Rabbi Zalman Schachter-Shalomi's early book *Paradigm Shift*, which looked at the collapse of the classical religions under the worldwide pressure of modernity —Rabbinic Judaism along with classical Christianity, Islam, Buddhism, Hinduism, Indigenous spiritual traditions, and other religious worldviews. And began looking beyond the collapse, hinting at the new forms of spiritual life that might emerge within, among, and beyond the old communities.

All these have been stewing in my kishkes, my innards, some for decades. Some aspects of my exploration came out in my earlier books. This is the first in which I have pursued them into the possible life-giving futures of the Spirit.

The present Board of The Shalom Center—Bob Brand, Cherie Brown, Rabbi Mordechai Liebling, Rabbi Lee Moore, Rabbi Jeff Roth, Rabbi Margot Stein, Linda Tobin, and Barbra

Wiener—and its program coordinator, Viv Hawkins, encouraged me to intertwine with urgent work in Torah-rooted activism and an urgent slew of arrests this longer-sighted view of what we might do with that urgency. It was Hazon's Isabella Freedman Retreat Center and specifically Director Adam Segulah Sher who opened their doors and their hearts to my taking weeks of quiet time in retreat, to turn my thoughts, still shaking in the great Earthquake, into coherent shape.

Phyllis Berman and the President Emerita of The Shalom Center, Arlene Goldbard, read the earliest maps of this exploration of the ancient past for the sake of a trembling future. They immeasurably improved the map.

Then it was Robert Ellsberg of Orbis who greeted his first reading after its appearance in his inbox with "I love it!" and has guided it through its journey into your hands.

* * *

My earliest and longest-lasting invitation to become an explorer came from my parents, Henry B. Waskow and Hannah H. Waskow; from my brother, Howard Waskow; and from the two children who grew up with me and with whom I have grown more up, David Waskow and Shoshana Elkin Waskow.

Next to them, in two clusters of my life, were first, my teachers of history, sociology, and activist engagement to make a new history and a new society: Professors Howard K. Beale and Hans Gerth at the University of Wisconsin; Congressman Robert W. Kastenmeier; Professor Kenneth Boulding at a month-long live-in symposium in Craigville, Massachusetts, sponsored by the American Academy of Arts and Sciences; and at the Institute for Policy Studies, especially Marcus Raskin as well as Paul Goodman, Leonard Rodberg, Barbara Bick, Frank Smith, Christopher Jencks, Ivanhoe Donaldson, and Charlotte Bunch. Second are those who taught me the joyful remaking of Judaism: Four giants, stretching across half a century—

Martin Buber, Rabbi Abraham Joshua Heschel, Rabbi Zalman Schachter-Shalomi, and Dr. Judith Plaskow.

In Jews for Urban Justice, Fabrangen, and the Fabrangen Cheder (a lay-led fellowship and a parents co-op school) where in Washington, DC, my work as a Jewish thinker–activist was first shaped: Rabbi Harold White, Mike Tabor, Rob Agus, Rabbi David Shneyer, Ken Giles, Rabbi Max Ticktin, Esther Ticktin, and Nessa Spitzer.

In the broader Jewish renaissance: Rabbi Everett Gendler, Everett Fox, Cherie Koller Fox, Rabbi Shlomo Carlebach, Rabbi Art Green, Rabbi Daniel Siegel, Rabbi Hanna Tiferet Siegel, Nessa Rapoport, Richie Siegel; Liz Koltun, Rabbi Laura Geller, Susannah Heschel, Rachel Adler, Marge Piercy, Rabbi Rebecca Alpert, Rabbi Linda Holtzman, Joy Ladin; Rabbi Michael Strassfeld, Joel Rosenberg, Rabbi Nancy Fuchs Kreimer, Dr. Barbara Breitman; Rabbi Mordechai Liebling, Rabbi Devora Bartnoff, Rabbi Jeff Roth, Rabbi Brian Walt, Jeffrey Dekro; Ira Silverman, Faryn Borella, Rabbi Shaya Isenberg, Bahira Sugarman, Larry Bush, Rabbi Sheila Weinberg, Rabbi Joanna Katz, Rabbi Julie Greenberg, Rabbi David Cooper, Shoshana Cooper, Ari Elon, Rabbi Michael Lerner, Rabbi David Saperstein, Rabbi Jill Hammer, Rabbi Susan Talve, Rabbi Naomi Hyman, Rabbi Gerry Serotta, Rabbi Marcia Prager, Maggid Melvin Metelits, Rabbi Shawn Zevit; Diane Levenberg, Marcia Falk, Marge Piercy; Hazan Jack Kessler, Cantor Jessi Roemer, Rabbi Shefa Gold, Joey Weisenberg, Cantor Linda Hirschhorn, Leonard Cohen; Sidney Shapiro, Micha Taubman, Paul Jacobs, Rabbi Arnold Jacob Wolf, Simha Flapan, Uri Avnery, Me'ir Pa'il, Dan Leon, Matti Peled, Rabbi Arik Ascherman, Sabri Jiryis, Issam Sartawi.

The Shabbat-morning Torah-weaving minyan at P'nai Or in Philadelphia, which gathers for an hour every week to weave our lives into Torah and Torah into our lives.

Those in the multireligious/multicultural/ethical-secular

communities active for the sake of justice, freedom, peace, and healing: Martin Luther King, Jr., Fannie Lou Hamer, Vincent Harding, Rev. William Barber, Rev. Channing E. Phillips, Rev. Bishop Marie Reed, Joyce Johnson, Rev. Nelson Johnson, Rev. Isaac Miller, Rev. Greg Holston, Bishop Dwayne Royster; Imam Al-Hajj Talib Abdur-Rashid, Sahar Alsahlani, Iftekhar Hussain; Elise Boulding, Kenneth Boulding, Viv Hawkins, Stewart Meacham, Ed Snyder; Starhawk; Allen Ginsberg; Sr. Joan Chittister, Dorothee Sölle, Rev. Joan Brown Campbell, Rt. Rev. Tracey Lind, Rev. Nancy Taylor, Rosemary Radford Ruether; Bill McKibben, Ted Glick, Rev. Matthew Fox; Rev. Cheryl Pyrch, Rev. Jim Wallis, Jean Stokan, Rev. Patricia Pearce; Rev. Richard Fernandez, Rev. William Sloane Coffin, David Dellinger, Will O'Brien, Deedee Risher, John Raines, Father Dan Berrigan, Rev. Rick Ufford-Chase, Rev. Bob Edgar, Father David Gracie; Tom Hayden, Carol Cohen McEldowney, Todd Gitlin; I. F. (Izzy) Stone, Teya Sepinuck, Gloria Steinem, Bella Abzug, Dr. Irene Elkin, Leo Szilard.

To these human teachers I add—

- a glowing cloud of fireflies in the Erev Shabbat dusk of a Pennsylvania farm called Licking Creek and Kibbutz Micah, that taught me that a glimmering of light in the midst of shadow may be as wise and true as bolder vision;
- the great Redwoods in California, which taught us that each one of us was a letter in the supernal invisible Torah Scroll held high by these astounding Torah-posts;
- and a Cat named Shadow who haunted a church and a synagogue in Philadelphia, seeking out sacred chanting and words of Torah and Gospel, and who killed himself by dashing grief-stricken into the path of an oncoming auto after he heard us talk of the murderous attack on the Tree of Life synagogue in Pittsburgh.

I realize that it may be frustrating to see these names without the stories of the moments when we learned with and from each other. Those tales will come—but that's another book, one I'm beginning as I finish writing this one: *Tales of the Spirit Rising*!

In Jewish tradition, we close a sitting together to learn wisdom with a prayer called the Kaddish. It begins by invoking "*Shmei Rabbah*, the Great Name." This "Great Name" encodes and invokes all the names of all the beings in the universe—especially the names of our teachers and our students.

May all who gather anywhere on Earth in any language to breathe together words that aim toward wisdom, and may we who have gathered just now to breathe together words that aim toward wisdom, as we finish reading this book and open our own hearts and memories to all we have learned and all we have taught, open ourselves as well to—

- the blessing of loving kindness as we listen to each other's diverse voices;
- the blessing of shalom, wholeness, as we begin to integrate what is new to us with what we have known before;
- the blessing of time to work for a decent, honorable livelihood made not from working on Earth's back or the backs of other human beings but as part of Earth and part of the human community;
- the blessing of time to pause from work, from Doing and Making, to reflect, to sing, to dance, to love, to Be; and
- the blessing of joining every breath and all our words in the great Breath of Life that is the Holy ONE.

Blessed are You, Interbreathing Spirit of the world, Who has filled me with life, lifted me up, and carried me to this moment!

Ameyn, amen, amin, may it be so!